BRITISH
PUBLIC
ADMINISTRATION

J. A. CROSS, M.A., B.Sc.(Econ.), Ph.D.

Lecturer in Politics, University College of South Wales
and Monmouthshire, Cardiff

LONDON

University Tutorial Press Ltd

9-10 Great Sutton Street, E.C. 1

Published 1970

SBN: 7231 0517 0

PRINTED IN GREAT BRITAIN BY UNIVERSITY TUTORIAL PRESS LTD, FOXTON
NEAR CAMBRIDGE

Preface

This book aims to give an up-to-date account of the machinery of British government. Fundamental changes in that machinery have recently taken place or are in immediate prospect: changes in Cabinet and departmental organisation, in the functions and structure of the Civil Service and of local government (enshrined, respectively, in " Fulton " and " Maud "), in the range of government agencies and in the techniques of administrative control. The book reviews these changes and places them in their administrative context. The emphasis throughout is on facts rather than opinions, but considerable attention is given to the analysis of problems of administrative structure. *British Public Administration* is primarily intended for use in professional or university courses in British government or public administration but should also be of interest to the general reader who wants a succinct survey of how his government is organised.

Contents

1. The Framework of Public Administration

Administration in the general sense is usually defined in terms of a co-operative human effort directed towards the achievement of agreed objectives. It is thus a social activity which can occur in a wide variety of institutional frameworks—a business firm, trade union, church, school, even a family. *Public* administration is administration in a political setting and, as distinct from private administration, is concerned with the formulation and implementation of public policy. There are features common to varying kinds of administrative organisation and much administrative theory is relevant to both public and private administration; but the distinguishing feature of public administration is that its activities are constrained by two linked if rather nebulous concepts: the public interest and public accountability.

The study of public administration involves description, the empirical examination of the structure and functions of the various parts of the governmental administrative machine. Can it be more than this? L. F. Urwick, among others, has criticised the fact that the considerable volume of literature on the working of various types of executive agency has, in the main, been historical and descriptive rather than analytical and critical and "appears to assume that the established practices in different countries represent a deposit of wisdom which it would be foolish to attempt to change". But how far can the study of public administration be *prescriptive*, laying down guidance for the creation and efficient operation of administrative organisations?

A theoretical approach to public administration obviously overlaps with general administrative theory. One of the first coherent attempts to formulate "principles of administration" was that made by Luther Gulick in 1937. Four techniques for achieving administrative efficiency were suggested: (i) specialisation of task among members of the organisation (i.e., specialisation); (ii) arrangement of the members in a determinate hierarchy (unity of command); (iii) limitation of the span of control at any point in the hierarchy to a small number (span of control); and (iv) grouping of the members of the organisation, for purposes of control, according to purpose, process, clientele or place (this fourth technique— the principle of departmentalisation—will be examined in Chapter 3). But, as Herbert Simon has pointed out, the principles conflict with each other (unity of command with specialisation, for example) and no guidance is given as to how they should be applied in particular situations. The "mechanisms of organisation influence" which Simon himself analyses—division of work, establishment of standard practices, transmission of decisions, channels of communication, and the training of organisation members—make no claim to be more than aids to description. In recent years interest (particularly in the United States, where most of the literature on the theory of public administration has originated) has concentrated on the study of *comparative* public administration. Highly sophisticated theories have been formulated (like the "prismatic theory" of F. W. Riggs) which claim empirical— and prescriptive—relevance to the problems of public administration, particularly in the developing areas of Asia and Africa.

It is understandable that much of the contemporary work on the theory of public administration should be concerned with new countries, since these have often to create administrative machinery virtually *ab initio*. But the great bulk of descriptive material is naturally based on the experience of advanced nations, which have developed administrative organisations over long periods, making changes only slowly in response to *ad hoc* situations.

Of no country is this more true than Britain. As has often been pointed out, the structure of British administration is chronological rather than logical. At no time has it been reorganised as a whole, but only partially as overpowering need seemed to demand. Thus the main lines of the Civil

Service were laid down in the third quarter, and the basic structure of local government in the last quarter, of the nineteenth century and it was not until the late 1960s that any fundamental reform of either seemed to be contemplated. Moreover, where apparent administrative innovation has been undertaken, as in the adoption of the public corporation model (already employed for broadcasting, electricity generation, and London transport) for the industries nationalised after 1945, the implications often seem not to have been fully worked out. The various parts of the British administrative machine are confusingly heterogeneous, ranging from the traditional ministerial department through various forms of semi-autonomous executive agencies (among them public corporations like the National Coal Board, regional hospital boards, the Industrial Reorganisation Corporation, and the Consumer Council) to the local government authorities, in form at least politically and administratively autonomous.

Many have seen in this long-term institutional inertia a basic cause of the relatively disappointing performance by Britain, especially in the economic field, since 1945. Until then the customary attitude to British political and administrative institutions had been one of complacency. British institutions were the norm, foreign institutions—like the American presidential system and French administrative law—were ill-understood divergences from it. The decline in Britain's world position since 1945 has, however, shattered this complacency. For Brian Chapman, writing in 1963, it is clear that "the institutions of British government have been signally unsuccessful in keeping pace with the modern world" and that Britain's decline as a Great Power has "probably been accelerated by her failure to provide herself with policy-making institutions adequate for the needs of the complex modern State". For Max Nicholson, a former senior civil servant, it was more appropriate to write in 1967 of the "Misgovernment of Modern Britain" than of its government since, above all, there was "no adequate and enduring provision . . . for studying existing or for anticipating future problems in public affairs, and for taking timely and sound dispositions to deal with them". From its two-year official investigation of the Civil Service the Fulton Committee, reporting in June 1968, concluded that the Service is "in need of fundamental change" since "it is inadequate . . . for the most efficient discharge of the present and prospective responsibilities of government". In the following year the Redcliffe-Maud Report declared that unless the local government system were reformed it would become increasingly discredited and gradually be replaced by central government agencies.

There is undoubtedly a greater readiness now than there was only a few years ago to examine institutions developed elsewhere (the Scandinavian *Ombudsman* being perhaps the outstanding example) with a view to their possible transference to the British environment. The decisions in 1966 to establish a British-style *Ombudsman*, or Parliamentary Commissioner (who started work in April 1967), and to initiate wide-ranging and high-level enquiries into the structure of the Civil Service and of local government have opened the possibility of institutional changes more fundamental in their scope than any for a century or more. The process may well be carried further with the establishment in 1969 of a royal commission to examine the constitution, and in particular the relationships between the various parts of the United Kingdom.

The contemporary concern with institutional reform is basically the result of disappointment with Britain's performance since the war. Had British policy, especially economic policy, achieved greater success the advocacy of, and need for, reform would have seemed less urgent. But it is not at all clear that a new form of administrative organisation will of itself solve the problem of which policy to choose or even how the chosen policy can best be achieved. An illustration of this would seem to be the general criticism of the role of the Treasury in shaping economic policy. Many felt that its restrictionist attitude, its concern with "candle ends" and the balance of payments, was inimical to planning for economic growth. As Harold Wilson put it a few months before he became Prime Minister in 1964, when balance of payments difficulties arise "the whole Treasury is pervaded with the idea that we must now hold down production". Thus when the Labour Government was formed in October 1964 an "expansionist" Department of Economic Affairs was created to balance the "restrictionist" Treasury. But there is little evidence to suggest that the quality of decision-making was significantly improved, and certainly economic crises were not avoided. Moreover, according to circumstantial reports in the Press when the decision to devalue sterling was announced in November 1967, the attempt to maintain the parity of sterling over the previous three years had been the result of the first major political decision taken by the leading members of the new government which the Treasury—and the Department of Economic Affairs—perforce had to accept (see Peter Jay, "Devaluation—who was to blame?" in *The Times Business News*, 23rd November, 1967).

It is impossible to separate politics from public administration and while institutional reform must continuously be undertaken it would be unwise to set too much store by it. The importation of analogies from business administration— the frequent call, for example, for a government of practical businessmen—is not altogether appropriate to the field of public administration. Cabinet decision-making cannot be equated with its business counterpart. The Cabinet is dealing with intangible, imponderable—often virtually insoluble— problems which are not susceptible of a simple profit and loss computation. If, for example, a government feels it has to make economies in public expenditure the decision as to whether, say, health service prescription charges should be re-introduced or orders for a military aircraft cancelled involve political and strategic decisions—in other words, considerations of the "public interest"—unlike anything met with in industry.

The main feature of public administration which differentiates it from other forms of administration—accountability to the public—itself has no necessary relationship to efficiency in the business sense. A more detailed measure of public control over administrative activity, while it may be desirable (since it may illuminate a particular interpretation of the public interest) will not inevitably make it more efficient. Control inhibits initiative and it is initiative which is often thought to be lacking in the administrative machine. This is the "dilemma of public accountability". It may well be, too, that the permanent personnel of the administration, above all that group within it that has most to do with policy formulation and advice, should be more representative of the social classes within the community which it serves. But this has nothing directly to do with increasing the efficiency of the personnel.

It is through the concept of ministerial responsibility that public accountability is formally achieved. Ministerial responsibility is of two kinds: the *collective* responsibility of all members of the government for the whole range of government policy and the *individual* responsibility of ministers for the conduct of their departments. It is the latter which is the more significant for public administration. Collective responsibility is a political fact, given the nature of the British party system, and simply means that the government, virtually secure in the support of their majority party members in the Commons, presents a united policy front, breached formally only when a minister resigns on policy grounds. Its fundamental basis is the unity of the parliamentary majority and as long as this is intact collective responsibility—at least between general elections—implies no method of external control. Individual ministerial responsibility does imply some sanction, however, although its exact nature is a matter of some controversy. In so far as individual responsibility is covered by collective responsibility—that is, that the government as a whole is prepared to back the individual acts (or failures to act) of one of its members—then the sanction is merely in the weakened form which applies in the case of collective responsibility. This would seem reasonable in the light of the nature of most governmental decision-making at the ministerial level. The great majority of top-level ministerial decisions are combined, rather than individual, operations, taken after a complex process of intra-governmental discussions.

But the individual nature of responsibility is preserved in form. Parliamentary statutes confer powers on individual ministers, not on the government as a whole. It is on individual ministers, not the government, that legal obligations are laid. It is a "Minister of the Crown", rather than the Crown itself, who can be sued in the courts if any servant of the Crown (i.e., a departmental official) has failed to fulfil a legal obligation or acted beyond his legal powers. The minister at the head of a department is thus legally responsible for the actions of all his officials in their official capacities. He is also politically responsible, in the sense that he is answerable to Parliament for all the activities of his department, many of them, in any case, involving ministerial *discretion* rather than legal obligation. The political doctrine of individual responsibility has often been held to include the sanction of the minister's resignation if a charge of mismanagement can be maintained against a minister himself or any of his subordinates. But, as will be seen in Chapter 7, while there are many precedents for ministerial resignation on personal grounds (as with Hugh Dalton in 1947 and John Profumo in 1963), those for "vicarious" resignations are much less clear. The main justification for the vicarious responsibility of ministers is the protection it gives for the anonymity—and hence the impartiality—of the permanent civil servants. But many see it as a barrier to informed opinion about what goes on in government departments rather than as an essential feature of British public administration. Thus Brian Chapman attributes to the doctrine "the principal reason why the British have been so reluctant to rationalise administrative institutions". And the initial opposition to such innovations as House of Commons specialist select committees and the *Ombudsman*, or Parliamentary Commissioner, would certainly seem to support this view.

Public accountability can be seen in wider terms than rather strictly delimited legal obligation and the political obligation of parliamentary question and debate. The tremendous increase in the responsibilities of government in the twentieth century, above all in the provision of comprehensive social services and the demands of central economic management, means that the administrative machine has to operate within a socio-economic-cultural context infinitely wider than had governments before 1914, or even those before 1939. There is now a complex intermingling of the public and

7

private sectors of the nation's economic life and the government thus has an intimate relationship with a whole range of organised groups or "publics", which need to be consulted on policy and whose co-operation may well be essential for its success. Nor can the process be confined to domestic organisations. There has been ample evidence in recent years of the extent to which British governmental policy-making has to be fitted in with international obligations. No longer are external relations the almost exclusive concern of a few departments, for they have increasingly to be taken into account by a whole range of traditionally "domestic" departments like those for the social services. Eventual membership of a supranational organisation like the European Economic Community would obviously accelerate the "internationalisation" of British public administration.

For Further Reading

Beloff, Max, *New Dimensions in Foreign Policy* (Allen & Unwin, 1961).

Chapman, Brian, *British Government Observed* (Allen & Unwin, 1963).

Chapman, R. A., "The Prismatic Theory in Public Administration" in *Public Administration*, 44 (1966), 415–33.

Fletcher, Peter, "Public Administration" in Wiseman, H. Victor (ed.), *Political Science* (Routledge & Kegan Paul, 1967).

"Fulton Report"—*Report of the Committee on the Civil Service 1966–68* (Cmnd. 3638, H.M.S.O., 1968). Chapter 1.

Gulick, Luther, "Notes on the Theory of Organizations" in Gulick and Urwick, L. F. (eds.), *Papers on the Science of Administration* (Institute of Public Administration, New York, 1937).

Heady, Ferrel, *Public Administration: A Comparative Perspective* (Prentice-Hall, 1966).

Nicholson, Max, *The System: The Misgovernment of Modern Britain* (Hodder & Stoughton, 1967).

"Redcliffe-Maud Report"—*Report of the Royal Commission on Local Government in England 1966–1969* (Cmnd. 4040, H.M.S.O., 1969). Vol. 1, Chapter XV.

Robson, William A., *Politics at Home and Abroad* (Allen & Unwin, 1967). Chapters 5, 6 and 8.

Simon, Herbert A., *Administrative Behaviour* (Macmillan, New York, 2nd. edn. 1957).

Subramaniam, V., "The Classical Organisation Theory and its Critics" in *Public Administration*, 44 (1966), 435–46.

Urwick, L. F., "Management and the Administrator" in Dunsire, A. (ed.), *The Making of an Administrator* (Manchester U.P., 1956).

Whitehall and Beyond (Broadcast interviews with Harold Wilson, Enoch Powell and Jo Grimond) (B.B.C. Publications, 1964).

2. *The Cabinet*

No part of the machinery of British public administration has been more critically examined than has the Cabinet. Argument is continual about what its role in the decision-making process was, is, or might be. Was it once a body of equal party colleagues under the impartial chairmanship of the Prime Minister? Has it now become a formal body, largely confined to ratifying decisions effectively made elsewhere—by the Prime Minister alone or by the Prime Minister in conjunction with other senior ministers? And in what institutional ways (if any) can the quality of top-level decision-making be improved?

Much of the difficulty in discussing the role of the Cabinet or of the Prime Minister derives from that necessary interrelationship between politics and administration to which reference was made in the last chapter. The Cabinet is above all a political organ and the relative standing of any of its members, the Prime Minister included, is largely a function of their position in the party. The view that the Prime Minister has now become a presidential figure (or, indeed, a supra-presidential one since, unlike the U.S. President, he can control the legislature through a disciplined party majority) seems to flourish at periods when the Prime Minister is clearly dominant among his parliamentary supporters, as was Lloyd George from 1916 until two or three years after the end of the First World War, Harold Macmillan between 1959 and 1961 and Harold Wilson from 1964 to 1966. The position of each of these leaders began to seem much less commanding as party support became less unanimous—and the dismissal of the once all-powerful Lloyd George (in what was admittedly the special circumstances of the ending of a coalition) was almost brutal in its suddenness. Much has been made of the Prime Minister's power of "hiring" and "firing" his ministerial colleagues, but although extensive, this power is not decisive. The balance of forces within the party must dictate many of the men to be appointed, even if the particular office is usually within the Prime Minister's complete discretion. There is no evidence to show that the most successful ministers are merely pliant office-seekers; indeed the outstanding members of Cabinets are precisely those who can demonstrate an independent strength. And if the *administrative* position of the Prime Minister *vis-a-vis* at least the more powerful of his colleagues is examined it is by no means necessarily one of dominance. Unlike senior departmental ministers he has no important executive department to brief him and is very much dependent upon advice from sources—the departments—which he cannot directly control. Indeed one of the most persistent themes in the perennial discussion of Cabinet reform is the need to provide an extra-departmental centre for decision-making intelligence, under the control of the Prime Minister on behalf of the Cabinet as a whole. In administrative terms the truth may be that the Prime Minister, far from being too powerful, is not organisationally equipped to be powerful enough. This kind of consideration may well have played a part in the Prime Minister's decision to take over direct responsibility for the Department of Economic Affairs for a period in 1967–8.

It is clear that the nature and scope of the decisions that have to be taken by the highest level of the administration has changed and developed over the past seventy years or so. The pre-1914 Cabinet, as J. P. Mackintosh has pointed out, was largely concerned with foreign policy questions, in which Britain, a great power with ample resources, had considerable freedom of action; with Ireland and the Empire; and with a small, if growing, number of domestic questions, mainly of a regulatory nature. Most policy decisions were implemented either by positive action in foreign affairs or by the passage of legislation enforceable by the courts. The necessity for consultation with powerful organised groups outside government was a relatively new feature of the administrative process. A generation later, the needs of economic management and the supervision of comprehensive welfare services were involving the government in close relations with a wide variety of interest groups, whose co-operation was often essential for the implementation of governmental policy. And the decline in Britain's world economic and strategic position has imposed similar restrictions on the government's freedom of action in international affairs. The fields in which decisions have to be taken have enormously increased while the autonomous power of a British Cabinet to take those decisions has sharply declined.

The process of expanding governmental functions has naturally been reflected in the composition of the Cabinet. By the beginning of 1969, after some years of intensive efforts to merge government departments (particularly since 1964), there were still nine departments which did not exist in any separate departmental form sixty years before: the Ministries of Transport, Power, Housing and Local Government, Overseas Development, and Technology; the Departments of Economic Affairs, Employment and Productivity, and the Civil Service; and the Welsh Office. Thus, in addition to the Prime Minister and certain other senior ministers traditionally without departmental responsibilities—like the Lord President of the Council, Lord Privy Seal, Lord Chancellor, the Chancellor of the Duchy of Lancaster, and the Paymaster-General—there were some twenty ministers at the head of government departments.

Until the formation of the wartime coalition government in 1915 it had been normal for virtually all full ministers to be included in the Cabinet. This was the case from 1902 until 1915 with both Conservative and Liberal Cabinets which, with a membership of twenty or twenty-one, comprised all full ministers apart from the Postmaster-General and the Law Officers (and even the Attorney-General, exceptionally, was in the Cabinet from 1912). During the First World War, and especially after the creation of a small War Cabinet in December 1916, many ministers, particularly those at the head of new departments (most of which disappeared when the war ended), were excluded from the Cabinet proper. The normal peacetime Cabinet system was re-established in 1919, with most ministers in the Cabinet, but from 1922 onwards a tendency to exclude ministers of the less important departments—such as the Post Office, Works and, for some time, Transport—increased. This was especially noticeable after the formation of the "National" Government in 1931. There thus arose a distinction between those ministers who were members of the Cabinet and other ministers who only attended Cabinet meetings when their departmental responsibilities were under discussion. One effect of this was to remove something of a barrier to the creation of new ministerial departments. As long as it was considered desirable both to keep membership of the Cabinet at around twenty and to include all ministers there was an obvious disadvantage in the proliferation of departments. But with the differentiation between Cabinet minister and non-Cabinet minister it was possible to retain a traditionally-sized Cabinet concomitantly with an increase in departments.

The Prime Minister now had the problem of deciding not only the allocation of portfolios but also whether a particular *man* or a particular *portfolio* should be in the Cabinet. On the one hand there will be pressures to have a Cabinet as large as possible in order to include all those with influential positions in the government party, to avoid friction between those included and those excluded, and to have the maximum representation of varied departmental views; on the other, administrative considerations such as the ease of summoning meetings, speedier decision-making, and the undesirability of taking ministers away from their departments more than can be avoided, might tend towards a small Cabinet. The balance struck by Prime Ministers since 1945 has ranged from sixteen in Churchill's 1951 Cabinet to the twenty-three in the Douglas-Home Cabinet of 1963 and the Wilson Cabinets of 1964 and 1968.

Some ministers will be included because of their office— either its intrinsic importance or the government's desire to demonstrate the importance it attaches to the work of a particular department—others because of their personal position in party or government. Since 1946, apart from the Prime Minister himself, ten ministers have *always* been members of the Cabinet: the Lord President, Lord Chancellor, Lord Privy Seal, Chancellor of the Exchequer, President of the Board of Trade, the Secretaries of State for Foreign and Commonwealth Affairs, Home Department, Defence (formerly the Minister of Defence), Employment and Productivity (formerly the Ministry of Labour), and Scotland. Since their creation in 1964 the Secretaries of State for Economic Affairs and for Wales have been in the Cabinet and seem likely to remain so; as no doubt will also the holder of the office of Secretary of State for Social Services created on the merger of the ministries of Health and Social Security in 1968. All these account, with the Prime Minister, for some fifteen Cabinet places. But the number of ministers capable of selection for the Cabinet who remain include such heads of departments as the Secretary of State for Education and Science (in every Cabinet, as Minister or Secretary of State, since 1953), the Ministers of Housing and Local Government (in every Cabinet since first appointment in 1951), Agriculture (in every Cabinet since 1954), Technology (in the Cabinet since establishment in 1964), Power (in the Cabinet since 1963), Transport (in the Cabinet since 1957), Public Building and Works, and Overseas Development, and the Postmaster-General. There are also ministers without portfolio like the Chancellor of the Duchy of Lancaster and the Paymaster-General. The Labour Cabinet at the beginning of 1969 had twenty-three members, leaving outside it three departmental heads (Public Building and Works, Overseas Development, and the Postmaster-General), the Minister for Planning and Land, Chancellor of the Duchy of Lancaster, two subordinate Ministers of Defence, and four Law Officers, and some twenty Ministers of State—an office increasingly used since 1943 to interpose a level between a full ministerial head of department and junior ministers (parliamentary secretaries or under-secretaries of state). (See Appendix, p. 182.)

The way in which the conflicting criteria of the "man" or the "office" may work in practice is demonstrated in the varying Cabinet fortunes of the Minister of Health and the Minister of Power (until 1957, the Minister of Fuel and Power) since 1945. When Aneurin Bevan was Minister of Health from 1945 to 1951—an important party figure introducing and implementing a fundamental piece of social legislation (the National Health Service)—the minister was in the

Cabinet. Bevan's Labour successor in office, a much less influential figure in the party, was excluded. For a short period at the beginning of the Conservative government which succeeded the Labour government in 1951 the Minister of Health (Crookshank) was also Leader of the House of Commons and as such was necessarily a leading member of the Cabinet But for ten years from 1952 a succession of ministers were all outside the Cabinet. Enoch Powell's promotion to the Cabinet in 1962, while still retaining the Health portfolio he had held since 1960, seemed a recognition of administrative ability and party standing rather than any increase in the importance of the department from the point of view of general government policy. His Conservative successor in 1963, although less well-known in the party, was also in the Cabinet. But from the time the Labour Cabinet took office in 1964 until the merging of the department with the Ministry of Social Security in 1968 the Minister of Health was not a member.

The Minister of Power has enjoyed similarly mixed fortune. Like Bevan, Emmanuel Shinwell, the Minister of Fuel and Power from 1945 to 1947, was a leading party personality ministerially responsible for important new legislation (that of nationalising the fuel and power industries) and as such a member of the Cabinet. But his successors from 1947 to 1957, covering both Labour and Conservative Cabinets, were all outside the Cabinet. When forming his Cabinet in January 1957 Harold Macmillan invited an old friend and former colleague, Lord Mills, to become Minister of Power, apparently, among other things, so that the Cabinet could have the benefit of his industrial experience. Lord Mills' successor, Richard Wood, Minister of Power from 1959 to 1963, was not in the Cabinet. But when, in 1963, F. J. Erroll was transferred to Power from the Presidency of the Board of Trade he retained his seat in the Cabinet. Labour Ministers of Power since 1964 have also been in the Cabinet, and this would seem to be primarily because of the importance attached (or desired to be seen to be attached) to the office rather than to the party standing of the minister.

The most obvious administrative consequence of the concomitant increase in governmental responsibilities and ministerial offices has been to increase the problems inherent in the co-ordination of government policy as a whole. Twentieth-century Cabinets have had to develop machinery either to relieve the Cabinet of some areas of decision-making altogether or to ensure that matters which need to come up for consideration in Cabinet are in as fully-digested a form as possible.

The Cabinet Secretariat

Much has been written of the informal and leisurely procedure with which nineteenth-century and early twentieth-century Cabinets conducted their business, without any formal agenda and without any record taken and transmitted, save for the private and personal letter which the Prime Minister wrote to the sovereign after Cabinet meetings. The consequence of this informality was, as Lord Curzon put it, that "The Cabinet often had the haziest notion as to what its decisions were ... cases frequently arose when the matter was left so much in doubt that a minister went away and acted upon what he thought was a decision, which subsequently turned out to be no decision at all, or was repudiated by his colleagues". Not surprisingly this primitive organisation proved inadequate to meet the exigencies of government when the country became involved in war from 1914, and a Cabinet Secretariat (or, at that time, *War* Cabinet Secretariat) was established in December 1916, when Lloyd George displaced Asquith from the leadership of the wartime coalition.

The new secretariat did not, however, spring fully armed from the fertile imagination of Lloyd George. It was a development of a pre-existing organisation and one which owed its origins to pre-war efforts to provide co-ordinating machinery for the drawing up of defence plans in the event of war. When the Committee of Imperial Defence was reconstituted in 1904 as an advisory committee to the Cabinet (unlike later committees its membership was not confined to members of the government), it was provided with a small permanent secretariat which kept the minutes and papers of the main committee and its numerous sub-committees. In

August 1914 the committee was virtually suspended for the duration of the war but its secretariat (under the leadership of the indispensable Maurice Hankey) carried on and provided secretariat services for the various organisational expedients the Asquith Cabinet experimented with before the formation of the Lloyd George War Cabinet in 1916: the War Council of November 1914, the Dardanelles Committee of June 1915, and the War Committee of November 1915. In addition the secretariat co-ordinated the activities of all Cabinet committees and of the many official committees which had proliferated from the outbreak of war; most of the secretaries of Cabinet committees were also assistant secretaries of the Committee of Imperial Defence. Thus even before the Cabinet had a secretariat its most important committees were using a common co-ordinating machinery. The War Cabinet Secretariat of December 1916 was in every sense the direct heir of the 1904 secretariat of the Committee of Imperial Defence and it was appropriate that the first Cabinet Secretary, Sir Maurice (later Lord) Hankey, should have been assistant secretary (from 1908) and then secretary (from 1912) of the Committee of Imperial Defence.

It was Hankey who in December 1916 drafted the first rules of procedure of the War Cabinet Secretariat and, with the substitution of "Cabinet" for "War Cabinet", they record what are still the basic functions of the Cabinet Secretariat:

(1) to record the proceedings of the War Cabinet;

(2) to transmit relevant extracts from the minutes to departments concerned with implementing them or otherwise interested;

(3) to prepare the agenda paper, and to arrange the attendance of ministers not in the War Cabinet and others required to be present for discussion of particular items on the agenda;

(4) to receive papers from departments and circulate them to the War Cabinet and others as necessary;

(5) to attend to the correspondence and general secretarial work of the office.

The wartime expedient erected on the basis of pre-war practice in the defence field was confirmed in November 1919, when the War Cabinet system officially came to an end and the Cabinet resumed its peacetime guise. Moreover the Secretariat which had, throughout the war, serviced the multiplicity of Cabinet committees as well as the War Cabinet itself, was explicitly charged, under instructions approved by the Cabinet in November 1919, to supply secretaries for Cabinet committees and "such Conferences as the Prime Minister may from time to time summon". In March 1920 the Treasury agreed to proposals to place the Cabinet Office— of which the Secretariat constituted the central core—on a permanent and established basis. An effort was subsequently made by Sir Warren Fisher, the permanent head of the Treasury, to subordinate the Cabinet Office to the Treasury (on whose Estimates, as a matter of administrative convenience, the costs of the Cabinet Office are borne) but Hankey was able to resist it.

The Cabinet Secretariat may have been accepted inside government, but it was not without critics outside government, however—despite the seal of approval that the independent Haldane Committee on the Machinery of Government had given to the device in its report published in 1918. Several speakers in a Commons debate in June 1922, including Asquith, argued that the Secretariat was unconstitutional. It conflicted with Cabinet secrecy and collective responsibility and—worst of all—it was the instrument used by the Prime Minister to dominate his colleagues. It was indeed clear from the debate that the real animosity to the Secretariat was on the mistaken ground that it interfered in the conduct of foreign affairs and constituted an important element in the personal government of Lloyd George. There was here an understandable confusion between the official Cabinet Secretariat and the unofficial group of advisers (the "Garden Suburb") that Lloyd George had assembled in his own personal secretariat at No. 10 Downing Street and which had infuriated official Whitehall, in particular the Foreign Office, by its activities on Lloyd George's behalf. At the election which followed the break-up of the coalition government in October 1922 Bonar Law, the Conservative leader, pledged himself to reorganise the Secretariat and restore to the Foreign

Office unequivocal responsibility for foreign affairs. When he took office after the election Bonar Law ended the Garden Suburb but retained the Cabinet Office and, with this acceptance by the first single-party government formed since its establishment in 1916, the Cabinet Secretariat may be said finally to have become an enduring part of the machinery of British government.

But the operation of the Secretariat was—and to a large extent still is—within carefully delimited boundaries, as the procedure for recording minutes illustrates. Hankey in 1918 described Cabinet minutes as "giving a general synopsis of the expert evidence on which the conclusion is based and a general summary of the arguments for and against decisions taken, preserving so far as possible the principle of collective policy". Views of individual ministers are not normally recorded unless it is considered necessary to give the opinion of a minister speaking with expert knowledge, or to give the details of the Prime Minister's summing up of a discussion. From August 1919 *minutes* became known as *conclusions*—a symbolic change, which aptly sums up the process. But the function is perhaps not always as entirely neutral as it appears. The determination of a precise conclusion after what may have been a ragged and inconclusive discussion may well involve some creative interpretation, especially if the Prime Minister as chairman has given no definite lead. L. S. Amery, who worked in the Secretariat during the First World War (and later himself became a Cabinet minister) found that "if one invented the best conclusion one could think of, it was rarely queried by those concerned"; a process which, in the Second World War, was once described as the secretary recording "what he thinks that they [the Cabinet] think that they ought to have thought". A former member of the Secretariat (Sir George Mallaby) has revealed that in 1953 Harold Macmillan jestingly accused the Secretariat of falsifying history since it gave the impression that the Cabinet was so intellectually disciplined that it argued each issue methodically and logically through to a set of neat and precise conclusions: "It isn't like that at all and you know it!" Another practice established almost from the very beginning was the recruitment of the

senior Secretariat staff—apart from the Secretary himself
and perhaps one or two of his chief assistants—by secondment
from the departments for relatively short periods only. This
has made the departments more willing to accept the Secretariat as a disinterested organisation, able to take an objective and impartial view of questions where departmental
interests conflict, since its staff, far from being an official élite,
are birds of passage between posts in ordinary departments.

The Secretariat's role in the preparation of the agenda
for the Cabinet and its committees is similarly a neutral one.
The inclusion of items for a particular meeting of the Cabinet
or committee is at the discretion of the Prime Minister (in
the case of the Cabinet) or the committee chairman. Under
the direction of the Prime Minister, the Secretariat tries to
ensure that the necessary preliminaries to the appearance
of an item on the Cabinet agenda have been gone through.
This may include the circulation of papers from the departments concerned (all policy papers with implications for
government expenditure—and few have not—must be seen
by the Treasury before circulation), while in the case of
draft legislation the Law Officers and, usually, the Treasury
are given the opportunity of commenting before general
circulation. Ideally some days (in the 1945–51 Labour
Cabinet it was two clear days) should elapse between the
circulation of papers and the appearance on the agenda of
the matter to which they relate—although this obviously
cannot be achieved when urgent matters arise, demanding
immediate attention. Ministers, including those not in the
Cabinet, are thus enabled to consider the items and, if they
wish, circulate written comments. The Secretariat will normally notify ministers outside the Cabinet when matters
involving their departmental responsibilities are to come up
and arrange for their attendance at the discussion. But the
circulation of papers gives a non-Cabinet minister who has
not been so notified but who feels that his departmental
viewpoint should be represented the opportunity to ask the
Prime Minister to be allowed to attend—a request which would
rarely be refused.

The Cabinet Secretariat, although it has expanded since

the early days, is still of relatively modest size. The original Committee of Imperial Defence Secretariat in 1904 consisted of a secretary and two assistant secretaries, but by 1917 the War Cabinet Secretariat had ten assistant secretaries under the Secretary. Forty years later the equivalent staff had increased only marginally—from eleven to about thirteen, including the Secretary, a deputy secretary, two under secretaries, two assistant secretaries and six principals. In recent years there has been some strengthening but the Secretariat staff still numbered only twenty-seven in 1969, when, in addition to the Secretary, there were three deputy secretaries, five under secretaries, eight assistant secretaries and ten principals.

The Cabinet Office also includes the Central Statistical Office, economic and scientific advisers and the Historical Section. The Central Statistical Office—an interdepartmental junction for the collection and analysis of statistics relating to the national economy—was one of two parallel creations of the Second World War. The other was the Economic Section which remained with the Cabinet Office until 1953 when it was absorbed by the Treasury, which thereby confirmed its monopoly of economic advice to the government as a whole. It was not until 1964 that a small staff of economic advisers reappeared in the Cabinet Office (accompanied by a similarly small staff of scientific advisers under the Chief Scientific Adviser to the Government). The Historical Section, whose origins go back to 1907, is quite outside the realm of policy advice. At first engaged on war histories only it is now maintaining a continuous record of departmental histories.

Although the Cabinet Office works closely with the Prime Minister—and is in some ways analogous, on a very small scale, to a Prime Minister's department—it is entirely separate from the Prime Minister's small personal Civil Service staff at No. 10, headed by an under secretary as Principal Private Secretary. Ever since the animus created by Lloyd George's Garden Suburb, Prime Ministers have been careful to maintain the distinction between the two entities although, of course, they have many points of contact.

Cabinet Committees

The Cabinet has long made use of committees to examine particular problems. In 1831, for example, the first Reform Bill was drafted by a Cabinet committee under the chairmanship of Lord John Russell. As the number of subjects within the ambit of government grew so did the practice of creating *ad hoc* committees to deal with them. At one Cabinet meeting during the great reforming Liberal Cabinet of 1906–15—in October 1911—three such committees were appointed, one to examine and report on Irish home rule, another on disestablishment of the Welsh Church, and the third on franchise reform. While this was not typical of Cabinet meetings at this period it was clearly not unusual. But until the Lloyd George War Cabinet in 1916 there were no standing committees of the Cabinet (apart from the special case of the Committee of Imperial Defence, which did not officially rank as a Cabinet committee). When he took office Lloyd George initiated an elaborate system of Cabinet committees, but with the re-establishment of the peacetime Cabinet in November 1919 only two of the standing committees remained: the Home Affairs Committee and the Finance Committee. The Home Affairs Committee had been set up in June 1918 to consider questions of home policy covering the work of more than one department that were of sufficient importance to demand Cabinet consideration. It had wide discretionary authority to deal with matters not involving major political issues without reference back to the Cabinet. But in its peacetime form it gradually became merely a committee to consider the current legislative programme and as such (normally under the title of the Legislation Committee) it has apparently continued in every subsequent Cabinet. The Finance Committee, set up in July 1919, considered questions of home and overseas policy involving expenditure as well as fiscal and budgetary policy. Although it continued beyond the break-up of the Lloyd George coalition in 1922 it does not seem to have become as firmly established as did the Home Affairs (or Legislation) Committee.

The coming of the Second World War led to the setting up of another highly complex system of Cabinet standing committees. But in 1945, unlike 1919, the system was continued in peacetime. A comprehensive system of standing and *ad hoc* committees is now a permanent feature of every Cabinet, with the choice as to number and composition in the hands of the Prime Minister, who is often chairman of the most important committees, leaving senior ministers without portfolio (like the Lord President), or sometimes the departmental minister most directly concerned, to chair the other committees. Committee membership embraces both Cabinet ministers and ministers outside the Cabinet and provides the major opportunity for the latter to participate in policy discussions in the broad field in which their departmental responsibilities lie (for meetings of the Cabinet itself they normally attend only that part of general policy discussions which directly affect their department). Even junior ministers may be members of Cabinet committees or sub-committees. In many cases the ministerial committees are paralleled by official committees, as with the Cabinet Defence and Oversea Policy Committee and the Chiefs of Staff Committee.

The committee system in any particular Cabinet is normally protected by a virtually impenetrable veil of secrecy. Public knowledge would, it is argued, militate against the doctrine of ministerial responsibility since, for example, the fact that a Cabinet committee on agricultural policy was known to exist would raise questions as to how far the Minister of Agriculture remained ministerially responsible in practice (a similar objection was made to the Churchill "Overlord" experiment in 1951, discussed below). The argument is not altogether convincing since it would be naïve to believe that a really major item of policy falling within the sphere of a particular departmental minister would be made by that minister alone, without consulting his colleagues and securing their assent. Thus the decisions to include a postponement of the raising of the school leaving age and the re-introduction of prescription charges among the economies in public expenditure announced in January 1968 were clearly taken by the Cabinet as a whole, not by the Secretary of State for

Education and Science or the Minister of Health alone (indeed, the "responsible" ministers may well have strongly resisted the proposals in Cabinet). It is difficult to see how the publication of information about committees would fundamentally affect the existing situation.

The existence of a Cabinet committee is in fact occasionally made known to the Press, and sometimes the name of its chairman—but never (with one exception) its actual composition. Thus, for example, an *ad hoc* committee on race relations was set up with the Home Secretary as chairman after the 1958 racial disturbances in London, Nottingham, and other towns, while the 1965 white paper on immigration policy was drafted by a committee under the Lord President. In recent years committees have been announced on such questions as the Common Market, Rhodesia, immigration, North Sea gas, and the nuclear power industry. In April 1968 the formation was announced of a Parliamentary Committee of the most senior members of the Labour Cabinet, responsible for reviewing the parliamentary and broader political aspects of the government's work.

The one exception to the general secrecy on the composition of committees is the Defence Committee or, as it has been known since 1964, the Defence and Oversea Policy Committee. This committee is, in a sense, the residuary legatee of the Committee of Imperial Defence and since that committee's membership was fairly widely known, so has that of its post-1945 successors. The Defence Committee, when it was established in 1946, consisted of the Prime Minister as chairman, the Minister of Defence as vice-chairman, and eight other members—the Lord President, Foreign Secretary, Chancellor of the Exchequer, Minister of Labour, Minister of Supply, and the three service ministers (the First Lord of the Admiralty and the Secretaries of State for War and for Air). There was a change in 1958 when it was announced that the Prime Minister would decide which of the members (who included three new members—the Home, Commonwealth and Colonial Secretaries—in place of the Lord President) would be invited to attend particular meetings—a practice reminiscent of the Committee of Imperial Defence.

In 1964 the newly-named Defence and Oversea Policy Committee was reduced to a "normal" membership of seven (compared with its predecessor's twelve): the Prime Minister, First Secretary of State, Foreign Secretary, Home Secretary, Commonwealth Secretary (an office since abolished), Defence Secretary, and either the Chancellor of the Exchequer or Chief Secretary to the Treasury.

In addition to the Defence and Oversea Policy Committee and the Legislation Committee (for current legislation) a modern Cabinet would presumably have standing committees to cover the other broad areas of governmental responsibility, such as economic policy, social services, other home affairs questions, and future legislation. The late Lord Morrison of Lambeth, a leading member of one post-war Cabinet—as Herbert Morrison he was Lord President and, for a short time, Foreign Secretary in the Labour Government of 1945–51—has given a fairly detailed picture of the committee system of that government and, while every Cabinet will have a somewhat different pattern, Morrison's account may be taken as reasonably representative of modern Cabinets.

Morrison lists sixteen standing committees as operating in the period 1948–51, following several changes in the committee structure in 1947. The committees covered: defence (chairman, the Prime Minister), civil defence (chairman, the Home Secretary), domestic policy not assigned to other committees (chairman, the Lord President and known as the Lord President's Committee, as was its wartime progenitor), economic policy (Prime Minister), production (Chancellor of the Exchequer), manpower (Minister of Labour), current legislation (chairman, Lord President and Leader of the House of Commons, and including the Lord Chancellor, Law Officers and Chief Whip), future legislation (Lord President), socialisation of industries (Lord President), machinery of government (Lord President), information services (Lord President), civil aviation (Lord Privy Seal), Commonwealth affairs (Prime Minister), China and South-East Asia (Prime Minister), Middle East (Foreign Secretary), and—a subject clearly thrown up by the immediate aftermath of war—policy towards liberated and ex-enemy countries. Some of the standing committees appointed sub-committees from time to time to examine particular topics within their field. In addition to the standing committees there were *ad hoc* temporary committees on such subjects as housing, the National Health Service, food supplies, and fuel (all four chaired by the Prime Minister), and civil service man-power and airfields (each under the Home Secretary).

Although Morrison does not disclose the precise com-position of the committees, his enumeration of the chairmen demonstrates the important part played by the Prime Minister and a senior non-departmental minister like the Lord Presi-dent in the committee system. Leadership at this level would seem to ensure that a committee would have a considerable degree of autonomous authority. If a committee is able to make agreed recommendations to the Cabinet they will normally be accepted (since the committee will include all the relevant departmental interests) and this procedure clearly saves Cabinet time by, in effect, decentralising decision-making. But in cases of disagreement at committee level there remains the traditional right of appeal of each depart-mental minister (including those outside the Cabinet) to the Cabinet itself.

Other Co-ordinating Devices

The committee system provides modern Cabinets with their main co-ordinating machinery. It is supplemented by a range of other devices, formal and informal. Of the informal techniques it is impossible, of course, to form any precise judgement. The balance of influence within the government will vary from Cabinet to Cabinet. The Prime Minister, necessarily enjoying a position of "exceptional and peculiar authority" (as Lord Morley, with much Cabinet experience, described it as long ago as 1889), will in most Cabinets be the chief individual co-ordinator, perhaps the chief initiator of major policies—although he will probably not normally be the completely dominant figure postulated by those who consider that "Cabinet Government" has been replaced by

"Prime Ministerial Government". In addition there will be some ministers considerably more influential than others, perhaps by virtue of their relationship to the Prime Minister or their chairmanship of important Cabinet committees— men like Bevin (Foreign Secretary), Morrison (Lord President), and Cripps (Chancellor of the Exchequer) in the Labour Cabinet from 1945. It seems unlikely that there is usually any very definite "inner Cabinet" of senior ministers but rather that the Prime Minister will consult different groups of senior colleagues on particular topics (though some may be in more than one such group). The small groups which, for example, supervised foreign policy in the Cabinet of Neville Chamberlain before the Second World War, planned policy towards Egypt after the nationalisation of the Suez Canal in 1956, or finally decided on sterling devaluation in November 1967, seem to have been "inner Cabinets" in this sense. The announcement in April 1968 of the setting up of a Parliamentary Committee of the Labour Cabinet gave rise to speculation as to whether in practice the new committee (which a year later was reduced in size) might become a more or less institutionalised inner Cabinet. On previous precedents, this would seem to be unlikely. It should be noted, however, that none of these devices necessarily displaces the Cabinet itself from its supreme co-ordinating role. No doubt the Cabinet often merely ratifies decisions effectively made elsewhere or at most arbitrates in cases of inter-departmental dispute—but nevertheless such action on its part is essential if the decision is to be implemented. But there will also be occasions on which the Cabinet itself reaches the final decision —as in recent examples widely reported in the Press at the time: the Wilson Cabinet's decision in December 1967 to maintain the embargo on the export of arms to South Africa; the prolonged Cabinet discussions which preceded the announcement of cuts in public expenditure in January 1968 and the 1969 debate on the so-called "penal clauses" in the government's proposed industrial relations legislation.

The need has sometimes been felt for additional co-ordinating machinery in specific areas, supplementing the committee system and other less formal techniques. An excellent illustration of the process is provided by the successive twentieth-century expedients to co-ordinate defence policy. They began with the establishment of the Committee of Imperial Defence—a purely advisory committee which did not affect the departmental autonomy of the service ministers, who remained important members of the Cabinet. In 1936 a "Minister for the Co-ordination of Defence" was appointed, but he had neither a department of his own nor formal authority over the service ministers (who remained in the Cabinet), and Britain entered the Second World War with no effective machinery for the co-ordination of defence policy. When Churchill became Prime Minister in May 1940 he took the additional title of Minister of Defence; but wartime defence co-ordination was achieved through the force of the Prime Minister's personality, the powers of his office, and the exigencies of war rather than through his assumption of a new ministerial title, especially as it was not supported by a separate department. Defence policy during the war was largely shaped by the Prime Minister and the Chiefs of Staff Committee, on which sat the professional heads of the three services. The service ministers themselves played a relatively minor role.

In 1946 it was decided that the time had come for the creation of a separate Ministry of Defence, under a minister who would have "both the time and the authority to formulate and apply a unified defence policy for the three services". He was to be responsible for the allocation of available resources between the services in accordance with the strategic policy laid down by the Defence Committee, under the authority of the Cabinet. The minister was the sole defence spokesman in the Cabinet, from which the service ministers were permanently dropped (although they remained members of the Defence Committee until 1964).

While in theory the new minister seemed to have overriding authority in defence matters things worked out rather differently in practice. In matters common to the three services—such as the provision of nuclear weapons (by the Ministry of Supply and, later, the Ministry of Aviation) and the administration of inter-service institutions—he had a direct influence, but he had no such direct voice in the detailed execution of defence policy by the service departments nor their administration of matters concerning one service only. The task was made no easier by the frequent changes of minister, most notably in the period 1955–6, when there were four Ministers of Defence in rapid succession. On at least three occasions—in 1955, 1957, and 1958—the powers of the minister were redefined without, however, any obvious effect on the position. Moreover, although the individual status of the service ministers had, with their exclusion from the Cabinet, clearly declined, there was no parallel decline in that of the professional service chiefs, for the Minister of Defence had at first no professional equivalent. But in 1955 a separate chairman of the Chiefs of Staff Committee was appointed and in 1958 he became Chief of the Defence Staff and chief professional adviser to the Minister of Defence; the individual Chiefs of Staff, however, in cases where they disagreed with their colleagues, preserved their long-standing right of direct access to the Prime Minister and Cabinet (which they still retain).

By 1963 it had become clear to the government that, in the words of its Foreign Secretary (the then Lord Home), "the existence of three major autonomous departments militates against the integration of defence policy which is our agreed aim", and from April 1964 the Admiralty, War Office, and Air Ministry ended their separate existence and were merged into a unified Ministry of Defence under a Secretary of State for Defence. The initial structure of the ministry was essentially tripartite, with a Minister of Defence at the head of each service échelon; it was not until 1967 that a functional organisation was formally introduced, under two Ministers of Defence—one for administration, the other for equipment— and the ministers at the head of each service were reduced to the status of junior ministers. It may well be that the combined ministry will never be completely viable until its internal organisation is wholly on functional lines, with no differentiated service elements (a reform which has already been undertaken in Canada).

The development of machinery for defence policy has

thus demonstrated at least three co-ordinating devices additional to the standing committee (which has been present in the defence field in one form or another since the establishment of the Committee of Imperial Defence) : a co-ordinating minister without department or specific powers; a co-ordinating minister possessing such powers and backed by his own department; and, finally, a combined department merging all the departments involved. There are clearly unique features about the defence field—of which the existence of three fighting services with their professional heads is the most significant—but there is no reason to believe that the defence experience is irrelevant to other governmental fields, and, indeed, there have been several parallel developments.

It was generally agreed that the appointment of a Minister for the Co-ordination of Defence in 1936 proved a failure. The minister had no power to take executive action and his co-ordinating functions were dependent upon the willingness of the heads of the executive departments to subordinate their departmental and service policies to the needs of a co-ordinated policy: there was no machinery to ensure this subordination. No one has described the inherent weakness of such a co-ordinating minister better than Winston Churchill, when he referred to "that exalted brooding over the work done by others which may well be the lot of a minister, however influential, who has no department"; instead of giving directions all he can give is advice, and instead of the right to act, even in a limited sphere, he has merely the "privilege to talk at large". It is all the more surprising that it was Churchill who, in forming his peacetime Cabinet in November 1951, was the first Prime Minister to follow the 1936 precedent and formally name certain non-departmental ministers for co-ordinating functions—although the arrangement was carried further since the ministerial heads of the departments to be co-ordinated, unlike the service ministers in 1936, were excluded from the Cabinet. Lord Woolton, as Lord President, was charged with co-ordinating the work of the then still separate Ministries of Agriculture and Food, while Lord Leathers similarly co-ordinated two departments as the cumbrously-styled "Secretary of State for the co-ordination of Fuel and Power and Transport". Churchill had also intended that there should be another co-ordinator in the economic field, to supervise—as Chancellor of the Duchy of Lancaster—the Treasury, Board of Trade, and Ministry of Supply, but his first choice for the post (Sir John Anderson, later Lord Waverley) refused the invitation and in the event no appointment was made.

During its brief existence the so-called "Overlord" experiment (a doubly appropriate term, as the two co-ordinators were both in the House of Lords) attracted a good deal of critical attention. While some saw it as an indication of how Cabinet organisation might well be developed many, including the Labour opposition in Parliament, with their recent ministerial experience, believed it to be unworkable—and it was undoubtedly significant (although not publicly known at the time) that so experienced and able an administrator as Sir John Anderson should have refused to participate in the experiment. The chief criticism was that the public announcement of the co-ordinators' functions blurred the ministerial responsibility of the departmental heads concerned in a way that the orthodox methods of Cabinet co-ordination—for example, by chairmen of Cabinet committees—did not. The result would be confusion in both Whitehall and Westminster, for the departmental ministers would no longer be in effective control of their departments or their staffs, while Parliament—to which they were supposed to be accountable—would have no means of telling where the responsibility of the minister ended and that of the overlord began. The actual responsibility of the overlords remained shadowy and apparently virtually immune from parliamentary enquiry. Moreover the fields to be co-ordinated in this way were much too narrow—a criticism which would presumably have lost some of its force if Churchill had been able to appoint an economic overlord.

Controversy about the experiment gained added impetus when, in a Lords debate in April 1952, Lord Woolton, in an unguarded moment, claimed that his co-ordinating responsibility was one he owed to the Cabinet, not to Parliament. The debates in both Houses which this statement provoked did not shed much light on the actual position of the over-lords and the ministers whose departments they were co-ordinating. Every departmental minister, Churchill affirmed, was responsible to Parliament for both the policy and the administration of his department, and this was not affected by the fact that non-departmental ministers had been named as co-ordinating the work of some departments. In exercising the latter function the overlords shared in the collective responsibility of the government as a whole and, as Ministers of the Crown, were accountable to Parliament. No informa-tion was given as to what direct contact, if any, the overlords had with the civil servants in the departments, or how far the departmental ministers had that automatic access to the Cabinet when their departmental responsibilities were under discussion which every other departmental minister outside the Cabinet enjoyed. Some indication of the personal diffi-culties involved was given when, at about this time, the Minister of Transport resigned on health grounds. Lord Woolton himself had to give up his co-ordinating duties (but not his membership of the Cabinet) for a similar reason later in the year and no successor was appointed. Lord Leathers resigned from office in August 1953 and this marked the final end of the experiment—less than two years after it had begun. It would seem reasonable to assume that the device had proved as unsatisfactory as had that of the Minister for the Co-ordination of Defence from 1936 to 1940, and for the same reasons—the overlords' lack of specific functions and firm departmental base.

The Labour Cabinet from 1964 again experimented with co-ordinating ministers but this time in one field only, and one which it seemed generally agreed required co-ordination—that of the social services. From 1964 to 1968 a non-depart-mental member of the Cabinet was named as having co-ordinating responsibilities for the social services and in April 1968 the Lord President of the Council was explicitly charged with arranging the merger (effected later in the year) of the Ministries of Health and Social Security, both under ministers outside the Cabinet, and with co-ordinating the social services generally. The extent of his control over other social service departments (e.g., the Department of Education and Science and the Ministry of Housing and Local Government) remained uncertain. (See Appendix, p. 182.)

The device of a co-ordinating ministry—like the Ministry of Defence from 1946 to 1964—has not been followed in other specific fields, although the Department of Economic Affairs, set up in 1964, has, like the Treasury (but without the Treasury's formal sanctions), been exercising general economic co-ordinating functions. The combined Ministry of Defence of 1964 had been anticipated in more restricted fields by the merger of the Ministries of Pensions and National Insurance (later the Ministry of Social Security) in 1953 and that of the Ministries of Food and Agriculture—Lord Woolton's former co-ordinating responsibility—in 1954. In 1966 the whole general responsibility for Commonwealth affairs was vested in one department, when the Colonial Office was merged with the Commonwealth Relations Office to form the Common-wealth Office. Two years later the "logic of events" was recognised and the new Commonwealth Office was itself merged with the Foreign Office. The merger of the Ministries of Health and Social Security in the same year (1968), under a minister with the title of Secretary of State for Social Services, may herald a similar rationalisation among depart-ments concerned with the social services.

The Reform of Cabinet Organisation

However unsuccessful—or limited in scope—the 1951–3 overlord experiment may have been it was an attempt to improve the organisation of the Cabinet to enable it to per-form its tasks more efficiently. The subject of Cabinet reform has been exhaustively discussed for many years—at least since the publication of the Haldane Report in 1918—although the impact of the discussion on the actual organisation of the Cabinet has been slight.

On the one hand, experienced administrators and minis-ters like Lord Waverley (Sir John Anderson) and Lord Morrison of Lambeth have testified that a traditionally sized Cabinet (of around twenty members), employing a coherent system of committees, should be fully adequate to the demands of modern government. But on the other hand, men with equal Cabinet experience (like Lloyd George and L. S. Amery) have argued that this pattern, which necessarily involves a departmentally-oriented Cabinet, is incapable of providing efficient inter-departmental co-ordination or— even more important—planning long-term policy. Ministers with heavy departmental duties—and these constitute the majority in the traditional Cabinet—do not have time to think about general policy except when an issue crops up so vital and urgent that it drives their departmental preoccupations into the background. They are not, in any case, encouraged to wander far from their departmental concerns, and this has been particularly true of foreign policy (for long almost the preserve of the Prime Minister and Foreign Secretary) and fiscal policy, where considerations of secrecy reinforce the dominant position of the Chancellor of the Exchequer. It does not seem, for example, that the Cabinet as a whole played any major part in the decisive stages of the 1956 Suez policy of the Eden Cabinet nor in the formulation of the July 1966 economic measures of the Wilson Cabinet (although it clearly played a bigger role in the 1967 devaluation crisis and the subsequent cuts in public expenditure). If ministers enter only at a late stage on discussions of current general policy beyond their immediate departmental responsibilities it would seem that *a fortiori* they do not normally participate in discussions of long-term policy. L. S. Amery, writing in 1935, described the "normal" Cabinet as being little more than a standing conference of departmental chiefs, where departmental policies are submitted to a cursory examination as a result of which they may be accepted, blocked, or partially adjusted to the competing policies of other departments. But each department for the most part goes its own way, fighting the "Whitehall War" to the best of its ability. A Cabinet so organised was, in Amery's view, incapable of handling "the complex and urgent problems of the twentieth century" since it provided for only mutual friction and delay, with at best "some partial measure of mutual adjustment between unrelated policies". Some support for Amery's contention was supplied by Lord Percy of Newcastle who (as Lord Eustace Percy) served with Amery in the 1925-9 Conservative Cabinet and recalled that none of its policy discussions could be regarded as adequate and in only one case did the Cabinet reject a strong recommendation from the departmental minister responsible—and that was a recommendation, at short notice, that it should modify a policy already adopted on the same minister's recommendation. There is no reason to suppose that the general situation in what is still primarily a departmental Cabinet has altered in any radical way since then.

The remedy has been found by many (but not by Prime Ministers forming peacetime Cabinets) to lie in smaller Cabinets, although whether this smaller body should include only non-departmental co-ordinating ministers, or only departmental ministers, or a mixture of the two, is not always made clear. The Haldane Committee in 1918 favoured a Cabinet of not more than twelve members, and preferably ten, but refused to pronounce on what kind of ministers they should be. Even two of the most sophisticated presentations of the reformist case—by Attlee in a book published in 1937, when he was Leader of the Opposition, and Amery, in his *Thoughts on the Constitution*, first published in 1947—are not completely clear about what should be the actual composition of the Cabinet proper.

In Attlee's view it was essential to make a distinction between ministers who are responsible for detailed administration and those "to whom is entrusted the work of dealing with the broader issues". The latter would be responsible for co-ordinating a particular group of services (Attlee specifies only four such groups: for the social services, defence, economic policy, and external relations) and would preside over a committee of ministers charged with the administration. The Prime Minister would thus be assisted in his oversight of the whole range of government policy, present and future, by "a small group of members of the Cabinet whose specific function is co-ordinating policy and giving general direction". Attlee was careful to say that the Cabinet would not be superseded nor departmental ministers relegated to an inferior status since the co-ordinating ministers would be in constant and close contact with the departmental ministers in their respective groups who would, through them, be able to make their views felt more effectively. But it is difficult to see how such a small group of policy co-ordinators could be anything other than an inner policy Cabinet, whether the full formal Cabinet was retained or not.

While there was some ambiguity in Attlee's 1937 position, Amery's seems quite clear—he wanted a "Cabinet of half a dozen, all entirely free from ordinary departmental duties". But this small Cabinet was to operate in two ways. It would have regular meetings for the discussion of future policy. It would also deal with "current administrative questions" by bringing into its discussions the departmental ministers directly affected, while members of the Cabinet would preside over standing and *ad hoc* committees of departmental ministers "with the advantage of their higher authority and of their freedom from other routine work". This sounds rather more like the traditional Cabinet pattern—with a comparatively large body discussing administrative matters and a system of Cabinet committees. Indeed, Amery later wrote that all he was concerned about was to have a definite group of policy ministers who had the principal authority in matters of general policy, and that whether they alone were called the Cabinet or whether that title was retained by a larger body including departmental ministers was "a matter of detail".

Although the advocacy of a small policy Cabinet continues unabated (recent proponents have included Lords Shawcross and Robens, both at one time members of the 1945–51 Labour Cabinet, and Max Nicholson, a former senior civil servant) the weight of opinion has been against such attempts to separate institutionally the policy and administrative functions of the Cabinet. Attlee's 1945 Cabinet was markedly different from his theoretical model of eight years before. Despite Amery's many years of Cabinet experience, it was generally felt that his attempted dichotomy between policy and administration was unrealistic. It did not take sufficiently into account the fact that ministers handling the actual work of administration must participate in the formulation of policy since much of it arises from the administrative process itself. Then there is the dilemma about responsibility. For a small group of policy ministers to accept full responsibility for the overall policy of the government would seem to impose an impossibly heavy burden upon them—but if they did not there would be no guarantee that the departmental ministers would in fact consent to being co-ordinated in this way. And, above all, such proposals ignore the dual nature of the Cabinet as a body of party leaders—"the focus of the chief politically articulated forces in a society" (Daalder)—as well as an administrative organ.

Nevertheless, although reforms along these lines have never been implemented there is a continuing and widespread concern that the Cabinet is in fact too departmentally-centred to be able to plan future policy efficiently. The information on which it has to base its decisions must necessarily come from the departments and by its very nature a departmental brief—or a conflation of departmental briefs— cannot constitute a general policy. The feeling that the formulation of Britain's economic policy since 1945 had been too much dominated by the Treasury was a factor in the creation of the Department of Economic Affairs in 1964, but the subsequent handling of Britain's growing economic difficulties, especially from 1966, does not suggest that this was a sufficient solution. Some see a central intelligence agency for the Prime Minister and the Cabinet as a whole—perhaps located in the Cabinet Office—as an essential prerequisite for adequate long-term planning. The Cabinet Office has been strengthened since 1964 and, as we have seen, now includes scientific advisers and economic advisers (the latter perhaps a belated recognition that the absorption of the former Economic Section of the Cabinet Office by the Treasury in 1953 was not altogether fortunate). But there are traditional constraints on the expansion of the Cabinet Office in the direction of a "super-department" serving the Cabinet as a whole, especially if the Cabinet remains—as it seems likely to do—primarily one of departmental ministers. As Mackenzie and Grove have pointed out, "a group of officials cannot serve

The Cabinet

collectively a group of ministers acting independently of one another, except in neutral matters such as secretarial duties and the co-ordination of statistics". Thorough-going reform of the Cabinet would seem to depend upon a re-examination of the departmental structure. (See Appendix, p. 182).

For Further Reading

Alderman, R. K., and Cross, J. A., *The Tactics of Resignation: A Study in British Cabinet Government* (Routledge & Kegan Paul, 1967).
Amery, L. S., *The Forward View* (Geoffrey Bles, 1935).
Amery, L. S., *Thoughts on the Constitution* (Oxford U.P., 2nd edn., 1953).
Attlee, C. R., *The Labour Party in Perspective* (Gollancz, 1937).
Brown, A. H., "Prime Ministerial Power" in *Public Law* (1968), 28–51, 96–118.
Chester, D. N., "Development of the Cabinet 1914–1949" in Campion, Sir Gilbert (*et al.*), *British Government since 1918* (Allen & Unwin, 1950).
Chester, D. N., and Willson, F. M. G., *The Organisation of British Central Government 1914–1964* (Allen & Unwin, 1968).
Daalder, Hans, *Cabinet Reform in Britain 1914–1963* (Oxford U.P., 1964).
Hankey, Lord, *Diplomacy by Conference* (Benn, 1946).
Heasman, D. J., "The Ministerial Hierarchy" and "The Prime Minister and the Cabinet" in *Parliamentary Affairs*, XV (1962), 307–30, 461–84.
Jennings, Sir Ivor, *Cabinet Government* (Cambridge U.P., 3rd edn., 1959).
Jones, G. W., "The Prime Minister's Power" in *Parliamentary Affairs*, XVIII (1965), 167–85.
Mackenzie, W. J. M., and Grove, J. W., *Central Administration in Britain* (Longmans, 1957).
Mackintosh, John P., *The British Cabinet* (Stevens, 2nd edn., 1968).
Mackintosh, John P., "The Prime Minister and the Cabinet" in *Parliamentary Affairs*, XXI (1968), 53–68.
Mallaby, Sir George, *From My Level* (Hutchinson, 1965).
Morrison of Lambeth, Lord, *Government and Parliament* (Oxford U.P., 3rd edn., 1964).
Nicholson, Max, *The System: The Misgovernment of Modern Britain* (Hodder & Stoughton, 1967).
Percy of Newcastle, Lord, *Some Memories* (Eyre & Spottiswoode, 1958).
Public Record Office, *The Records of the Cabinet Office to 1922* (H.M.S.O., 1966).
Whitehall and Beyond (B.B.C. Publications, 1964).
Wilson, Harold, "The Machinery of Government" (interview with Norman Hunt) in *The Listener*, 6th and 13th April, 1967.

3. Government Departments: Distribution of Responsibilities

The ministerial department is the nodal point of the British administrative system. Directly or indirectly all parts of the administrative machine, however autonomous in form, are linked with a minister responsible to Parliament for a department staffed by permanent civil servants. This applies equally to government departments specifically headed by ministers, to departments which have no ministerial head (but for all of which some minister is responsible, as the Chancellor of the Exchequer is for the Boards of Inland Revenue and Customs and Excise), and to semi-autonomous bodies like public corporations for which a minister will have ultimate responsibility even if it is not formally so wide-ranging as for his government department. It is through the agency of government departments that government policy is formulated and implemented.

As with so much else in the British governmental system the "Departments of State" have developed, not as part of a coherent plan, but in response to historical circumstances. The present Secretaries of State, for example, are descended from the medieval King's Secretary and constitutionally all are equally responsible for executing the royal commands. In practice, of course, each of the modern Secretaries of State is the head of a separate department, like the Foreign and Commonwealth Office, Home Office or Department of Education and Science. The former Admiralty—which was absorbed into the Ministry of Defence in 1964—had been the successor to the Lord High Admiral, the Treasury to the Lord Treasurer. Some departments—for example, those for agriculture and education—originated as committees of the Privy Council (the Board of Trade is still nominally controlled by a "board" or committee). Others have been hived off from existing departments, as the Ministry of Labour (now the Department of Employment and Productivity) separated from the Board of Trade in 1916 or the Dominions (later Commonwealth) Office from the former Colonial Office in 1925. The former Local Government Board, formed from the fusion of the Poor Law and Public Health Boards in 1871, gave rise to the Ministry of Health in 1919 and, indirectly, to the present Ministries of Transport and Housing and Local Government.

Since the first use of the term in 1915 the most common formal designations for a department and its political head has been "Ministry" and "Minister", while both titles are also used generically (thus the Board of Trade, as well as the Ministry of Agriculture, is referred to as a "Ministry"). From the First World War onwards there has been an absolute increase in the number of departments but within this general process, functions have been transferred and departments come and gone with remarkable frequency without, it may be added, noticeably improving the coherence or rationality of the overall departmental pattern. The Ministry of Supply, for example, was established immediately before the Second World War but twenty years later (in 1959) was disbanded and its major functions taken over by the Ministry of Aviation, which itself was absorbed by the Ministry of Technology in 1967. The Ministry of Town and Country Planning, set up in 1942, eventually became the Ministry of Housing and Local Government in 1951 after housing responsibilities had been transferred from the Ministry of Health. The Ministry of Land and National Resources—which at the beginning of its existence in 1964 was worsted in a conflict over town and country planning responsibilities with the Ministry of Housing and Local Government—was absorbed by that department a little over two years later. The Whitehall pattern has been determined more by political considerations than administrative logic.

Are there, nevertheless, any theoretical principles for allocating departmental responsibilities? The Haldane Report of 1918 discussed only two: major function and clientele. The former leads to great functional departments like Health, Transport, Employment and so on; the latter to ministries of old people, or children, or for particular industries. There is no clear example of the clientele principle in Whitehall but, in a sense, the Ministry of Agriculture is a ministry of farmers and the Department of Education and Science partly a ministry of schoolchildren; while the Children's Department of the Home Office has wide responsibilities for children in need of care or protection. Certain "production" departments sponsor and act as the main governmental point of contact for major industries (e.g., the Ministry of Technology and the mechanical and electrical engineering industries, etc.).

Gulick's 1937 "principles of administration" (to which reference was made in Chapter 1) added "work process" and "place" to the two Haldane principles. Work process would involve ministries of doctors, engineers and so on and is seen in Whitehall only in the form of governmental common service departments, like the Stationery Office (government printing), Central Office of Information (advice on publicity techniques), and the Ministry of Public Building and Works (works services). Organisation by place is seen in the internal organisation of government departments (e.g., regional and local offices) but rarely as a separate department—although the Scottish and Welsh Offices and the former Colonial Office are obvious examples of the process.

The Haldane Report came down heavily in favour of the functional principle. The "inevitable outcome" of organisation by clientele was, the Report said in a famous phrase, "a tendency to Lilliputian administration". When, as in organisation by clientele, the work of a department "is at the same time limited to a particular class of persons and extended to every variety of provision for them" it is impossible for it to be "of as high standard" as when a department "concentrates itself on the provision of one particular service only [i.e., major function] by whomsoever required and looks beyond the interests of comparatively small classes". Gulick also favoured the same principle since "organisation by major purposes serves to bring together in a single department all of those who are at work endeavouring to render a particular service". But there are several difficulties in the concept. It rests on the unproven—and probably unprovable— assumption that (to quote Herbert Simon) "a child health unit, for example, in a department of child welfare could not offer services of 'as high a standard' as the same unit if it were located in a department of health". The way in which the transfer of such a unit from one department to another would improve or damage the quality of its work is left unexplained. Moreover, while (as W. J. M. Mackenzie has pointed out) the allocation of departmental responsibilities by functions rather than persons to be served may be convenient for administrators it is not necessarily so convenient for the general public, for whom a single office capable of handling all the business brought to it by a particular group may be preferable to the possibility of having to go on circuit through a series of different offices. It was significant that a good deal of opposition was expressed to the merger in 1953 of the Ministry of Pensions with the Ministry of National Insurance since the former department had from its creation in 1916 established an excellent record of concern for the interests of war pensioners and their dependents in ways beyond the purely financial and it was feared that this concern would be lost in the larger department.

But the most serious difficulty is that of demarcating functions or services. What is a particular service? Simon asks, "Is fire protection a single purpose, or is it merely a part of the purpose of public safety? Or is it a combination of purposes including fire prevention and fire fighting?" He concludes that there is no such thing as a unifunctional organisation, and this is certainly borne out in Whitehall where even the clearly functional departments like Health (now part of

a merged department) and Education share some functions
with others: Health, with Housing (public health), Employment (health in factories), Defence (Forces' medical services),
Education (school health service), and the Scottish and Welsh
Offices; Education which, in addition to its overlap with Health,
shares functions with Defence (Forces' education), Employment (industrial training), Scottish Office (Scottish Education
Department). For long the Ministry of Agriculture was responsible for agricultural education and the Ministry of Health for
the education of mentally-handicapped children: the functions
were not transferred to the Department of Education and
Science until 1964 and 1968, respectively. The problem of
allocating functions in the defence field has already been discussed (Chapter 2) and the examples that follow illustrate the
same difficulty in other important spheres of governmental
responsibility.

Treasury Functions

There is no better illustration of the complexity of the
problems posed by the rational allocation of functions to
departments than the role played by the Treasury in British
government. The Treasury is unique: if it did not exist
it would be virtually impossible to invent it. Starting in
the relatively humble role of supervisor of revenue collection
and governmental expenditure its status inevitably rose as
governmental responsibilities—and with them expenditure—
increased and as the fiscal and monetary functions which the
Treasury exercised came to be accepted as important tools of
governmental influence over the economy. Treasury control
over departmental expenditure extended to control over
departmental establishments since, when governmental responsibilities were limited, expenditure on staff was always a
significant—and sometimes the most important—item in
departmental expenditure. With the acceptance of governmental responsibility for general economic management
(often dated from the publication of the White Paper on Full
Employment in 1944) the Treasury seemed the obvious
department to exercise general co-ordinating powers. Thus

the Treasury was, in effect, a ministry of finance, a ministry of economic co-ordination, and a ministry of the Civil Service at one and the same time: in no other governmental system were so many crucial co-ordinating functions performed by a single department. This concentration of power within the Treasury, not surprisingly, found many critics.

Perhaps the most controversial Treasury function has been that of co-ordinating economic policy, of attempting to ensure that "the various functions of government in the economic field are carried out in a related way with the objective of keeping the economy on an even keel, its resources fully employed, yet with inflationary pressures kept in check" (Sir Eric Roll). At one stage after the Second World War, until Sir Stafford Cripps became Chancellor of the Exchequer in 1947, it looked as if the Treasury might not become the chief department for economic management. Herbert Morrison, as Lord President of the Council, had important co-ordinating functions in the economic field until July 1947 when for a few months Cripps, as Minister for Economic Affairs, controlled the activities of the newly-created central economic planning staff. But before 1947 was out Cripps himself became Chancellor and took the planning staff and his co-ordinating functions into the Treasury with him. In 1953 the former Economic Section of the Cabinet Office was also absorbed into the Treasury. An important Treasury reorganisation in 1962 was designed to equip it to perform its functions more effectively. One of the joint permanent secretaries, as official Head of the Home Civil Service, headed two groups dealing with the pay and management of the public service, while the other controlled the financial and economic policy side of the Treasury, with groups dealing with finance, public expenditure and resources, and the national economy.

But the feeling was growing that the Treasury was not the appropriate department to deal with the detailed supervision of economic policy. In part it arose from doubts whether the Treasury, with all its newer functions to discharge, was adequately performing its traditional role of "national housekeeping", of supervising public expenditure (doubts which had led to the establishment of the Plowden

Committee on the control of public expenditure), which in many administrative systems is considered a responsibility of sufficient importance to justify a department to itself (e.g., the U.S. Bureau of the Budget). It was argued, too, that the necessity of preparing the annual Budget inevitably limited the Treasury to a one-year time horizon, a period far too short for successful economic planning. And others thought that however the Treasury might be reorganised internally (and the 1962 changes were clearly far-reaching) it would still necessarily be pre-occupied with the state of the balance of payments and the level of the gold reserves. Treasury influence was thus inevitably deflationary and inimical to an economic policy in which insistence on sustained economic growth was a prime requirement.

Such arguments may have played a part in the decision by the Conservative Chancellor of the Exchequer, Selwyn Lloyd, to set up in 1962 the National Economic Development Council. The Council itself was in the traditional mould of a government consultative committee representative of industrial management and the trade unions, although the number and status of its ministerial membership was unusual in such bodies. The unique feature was the appointment of a staff to service it, under a Director-General, independent of the Civil Service machine (the National Economic Development Office).

Despite its independent source of advice in N.E.D.O. the Council could still essentially perform only an advisory role. Its creation thus hardly satisfied those critics who believed that the Treasury was constitutionally unable, through its "obsession" with balance of payments problems, to superintend a policy for economic growth. Harold Wilson, the new Leader of the Labour Party, for example, adumbrated at the party's 1963 conference a new ministry of production and/or planning which would be responsible for co-ordinating decisions about expansion in the physical field and deciding what industries needed to be encouraged, by fiscal or other means. Soon afterwards Edward Heath was appointed, in the new Douglas-Home Cabinet, as "Secretary of State for Industry, Trade and Regional Development" to preside over an expanded Board of Trade. The Treasury retained general responsibility for economic planning (the *macro*-economic field) while the new Board of Trade concerned itself with the economic efficiency of particular industries and regions (the *micro*-economic field).

When the Labour Government was formed in October 1964 the projected "minister for production or planning" became "Secretary of State for Economic Affairs", in charge of a small department—the Department of Economic Affairs—recruited mainly from the national economy group of the Treasury and some of the staff of N.E.D.O. The stimulus for this organisational change was fourfold: the belief that the traditional fiscal and monetary weapons operating over the economy as a whole needed to be supplemented by others; the wide disparities which existed between economic conditions of different parts of the country; the relatively slow growth in Britain's industrial productivity compared with its industrial competitors; and, above all, the belief that the recurring balance of payments crises originated in structural deficiencies in the economy. The main objective of the new department was (according to its first permanent head, Sir Eric Roll) "to co-ordinate the activities of the economic departments of government so that their decisions are consistent with the achievement of a faster rate of growth while avoiding inflationary pressures; and through ... relations with both sides of industry to secure a wide acceptance of the need to change our approach towards those factors in our economic life which impede economic growth". It was an objective in which other departments—notably the Treasury, Board of Trade, and the Ministries of Labour (as it then was), Technology, Power, Transport, Housing and Local Government, Public Building and Works, and Agriculture—were also involved. But unlike these other departments the D.E.A. had no executive responsibilities, no narrow departmental interest to defend but was (to quote Sir Eric Roll again) "concerned with the welfare of the economy as a whole".

The department with which there was the greatest overlap was, of course, the Treasury. The D.E.A. was principally interested in the longer-term problems of the use and development of physical resources, while the Treasury was mainly, though not exclusively, concerned with the shorter-term problems of public expenditure, taxation, and finance. Both, however, were essential to economic policy and there had to be a very close working relationship between the two departments.

The experience of the new department was not altogether happy. Much of its early effort was devoted to securing industrial co-operation in a voluntary incomes and prices policy and in drawing up an ambitious National Plan projecting the growth of the economy over the next five years. Both were overtaken by the economic crisis of July 1966. As difficulties increased and as the inevitability of sterling devaluation (sixteen months later) came to be accepted the D.E.A. necessarily played a markedly junior role to the Treasury, whose monetary and fiscal weapons were once again called in to play to cope with the situation. The D.E.A.'s macro-economic role appreciably declined. Co-ordination of overseas economic policy was transferred to the Board of Trade in August 1967 and in April 1968 the D.E.A. also lost its function of supervising the now statutory prices and incomes policy to the Ministry of Labour, under its new title Department of Employment and Productivity. It came increasingly to concentrate on industrial efficiency and regional economic planning. This was a field in which the Board of Trade and the Ministry of Technology were also intimately involved, and some commentators urged that it would organisationally have been more sensible to have a ministry of industry which would concentrate in itself the various industrial responsibilities of the departments. At the same time overall economic policy might once again be the responsibility of a single department, born of a merger of the D.E.A. and the Treasury. Clearly the creation of the D.E.A. had not solved the functional problems inherent in the way the Treasury had developed. (See Appendix, p. 182.)

The third major function of the Treasury—that of Civil Service management (the word now officially preferred to the traditional "control")—also came under criticism. The Plowden Committee on the control of public expenditure, reporting in 1961, took it for granted that the function would remain with the Treasury but the case for separating it was apparently officially considered at the time of the 1962 re-organisation, only to be rejected. The transfer of the responsibility, either to the Civil Service Commission—the independent body responsible for recruiting permanent civil servants—or elsewhere, has, however, continued to be urged. Then, in June 1968, came the recommendation of the Fulton Committee, immediately accepted by the government, that a new Civil Service Department should be established under the Prime Minister (assisted by another member of the Cabinet) to take over and extend the Treasury's central responsibility for Civil Service staff matters and the Civil Service Commission's function of impartial recruitment to permanent posts. The committee did not consider that central Civil Service management was an appropriate function for the Treasury as the central finance department since:

(1) the role of central management needed to be enlarged and if this enlarged responsibility were to be added to the Treasury's responsibilities for financial and economic policy and for the control of public expenditure, there would be reason to fear too great a concentration of power in one department;

(2) the pay and management side of the Treasury was staffed by those whose main training and experience had been in techniques of government finance and the control of expenditure, rather than in personnel work;

(3) central management should be positively and creatively concerned with maintaining and improving Civil Service standards. "It should therefore (the committee thought) be a separate institution with a single-minded devotion to its own professional purpose; and should be in a position to fight, and to be seen fighting, the Treasury on behalf of the Service."

But the committee recognised that it would be important to ensure that the functions of the new department and of the Treasury and the relationship between them was clear and distinct, and that the Civil Service Department had "a real base of independent authority without impairing the ultimate authority of the Treasury and the Chancellor of the Exchequer for the control of public expenditure as a whole". The Treasury should, for example, retain its existing concern for the total cost of particular services which would include, in varying proportions, the cost of employing civil servants; but it would be for the new department, rather than the Treasury, to determine the scale of staffs necessary for the efficient discharge of the tasks of departments. If the Treasury took the view that the total expenditure should be reduced, it would be free to challenge the policies of the spending departments, but not the assessment of staff costs approved by the Civil Service Department. It remains to be seen whether the committee's objective of "the clearest possible distinction between the functions and responsibilities of the two central departments" can be achieved in practice. What is clear, however, is that the committee felt that the Treasury was partly responsible for the defects it discovered in the central management of the Civil Service by failing to keep the Service up-to-date. As with the Department of Economic Affairs, so with the new Civil Service Department (established in November 1968), the solution was seen to lie in a new distribution of departmental responsibilities.

Higher Education

The Treasury was also for long directly involved departmentally with an important aspect of higher education (the universities), on which the Robbins Committee reported in October 1963. The publication of the Robbins Report, among other things, sparked off a hotly-contested debate on the appropriate departmental arrangements for higher education, and the university sector within it in particular. At the time the committee was deliberating the universities—autonomous chartered institutions—dealt direct with the Treasury through the mediation of the University Grants Committee, an independent body representative of university interests. The ten colleges of advanced technology—which the committee recommended should be given university status—were administered by the Ministry of Education (as it then was) on a direct grant basis. Most of the other institutions of higher education—teacher training colleges and technical colleges— were directly administered by local education authorities subject to general guidance from the Ministry of Education. The Research Councils (e.g., the Medical Research Council and the Agricultural Research Council), which had close research and financial links with universities, were the responsibility of the Lord President of the Council (who had the additional title of Minister for Science and as such was assisted by a small office).

The Robbins Report envisaged the colleges of advanced technology and also perhaps some other advanced colleges becoming universities, close links between the teacher training colleges (to be renamed colleges of education) and universities, and a great expansion in student numbers in universities as in other institutions of higher education. The annual Treasury grant to universities, already standing at £100 million, was obviously going to increase substantially. The committee therefore thought it incumbent upon it to examine the question of what governmental machinery would be appropriate in future for co-ordinating the greatly enlarged autonomous university sector. It considered four possible alternatives: (i) the extension of the existing Treasury responsibility over the whole expanded university field; (ii) the transfer of responsibility to the Lord President or some other minister without portfolio; (iii) the transfer of *all* higher education responsibilities, including those for universities, to the Ministry of Education; (iv) the creation of a new ministry for universities, together with other autonomous bodies. The arguments the committee deployed for and against these alternatives provide an excellent illustration of the difficulties of determining a clearly defined function for the purposes of departmental organisation.

The first alternative was never really a runner since the Treasury in evidence to the committee had indicated that it would not be prepared to take over responsibility for the colleges of advanced technology elevated to university status. And even as regards existing universities Treasury officials were themselves "more and more conscious of the anomaly of a state of affairs in which they, whose normal function it is to be guardians of the public purse, in this capacity are claimants upon it". The Treasury seems in fact to have been anxious to remove the increasing danger that it would become, in the rapidly-expanding university field, a considerable "spending department" itself. Nor did the committee spend long on the idea of a minister without portfolio. If he were to remain as such he would be able to have only a small personal office which, even though it would be assisted by the University Grants Committee and its staff, would be incapable of performing adequately the continuous and important function of "assessing the advice received and presenting claims in competition with claims from other departments".

The case for the Minister of Education (with the new title of Secretary of State) assuming responsibility for universities is examined in more detail. Among the "weighty arguments" in favour of this solution was the fact that it would facilitate a unified survey of educational problems in all their aspects, would involve unified control, and would tend to encourage a sense of common purpose among all engaged in various parts of the educational system. Moreover, there was the good administrative record of the Ministry of Education: "Any fair observer must admit that, in forwarding the various branches of higher education with which it has been concerned, its record has been outstanding."

Nevertheless the committee as a whole (with one dissentient) rejected the solution of amalgamating all responsibility for education under one minister. In the first place, it considered the area of responsibility too wide. The methods and problems of higher education differed considerably from those in school education and needed separate departmental supervision. There was a danger that both kinds of education would receive less attention than they deserved if they were the responsibility of one minister and ministry rather than two. The committee's second objection concerned "matters of administrative style". The co-ordination of autonomous institutions through a grants committee involved the preservation of a "delicate balance" and consequently very different administrative methods from those required else-where in the educational system. Thirdly, the concern of the main institutions of higher learning with the advancement and preservation of knowledge, as well as with education, meant that their organic connections were closer with other forms of research than with the work of the schools—connections which would be lost if their co-ordination were entrusted to the Ministry of Education (the Trend Report on the organisation of civil science, also published in October 1963, had agreed that "there would be obvious advantages in an arrangement whereby responsibility for higher education and responsibility for civil scientific policy were vested in one and the same Minister").

Having thus argued against a single Ministry of Education the committee might have been expected to recommend a separate ministry of higher education, supervising universities, colleges to be elevated to university status and other institutions of higher education whose work was obviously more analogous to that of universities than of schools. But it did not do so. Technical and other further education colleges were to remain with local education authorities and thus be supervised by the Ministry of Education. The committee proposed the creation of a "ministry of arts and sciences" responsible for a more limited range of institutions of higher education—in fact for *autonomous* institutions, suitable for control on the grants committee principle. These would include not only the universities (new and old) but also the Research Councils (and the other responsibilities of the Minister of Science), the Arts Council and other bodies designed to forward learning and the arts, such as the Standing Commission of Museums and Galleries. "In this way", the committee claimed, "an administrative recognition would be given to the essential unity of knowledge; and the nature of the administrative tasks involved would be such as to blend well in a common departmental tradition. Since much of the work would be done through grants committees, the whole would tend to be informed by the special degree of detachment and respect for the autonomy of the institutions and individuals ultimately concerned that is so necessary if the connection of the State with creative activities is to be a quickening rather than a deadening influence." The contribution which the autonomous institutions had to make was so important that it must have separate articulation. If there were only one ministry of education as a whole the right of appeal in the event of conflict would be within the walls of the department only, but with two ministers it would go to the Cabinet or at least a Cabinet committee. It was "this possibility of independent appeal from the ruling of a single minister to the supreme policy-making authority" which the committee regarded as "an essential guarantee of the status and liberties of the autonomous institutions".

Reaction to this particular recommendation of the Robbins Report was predictable. The teaching profession and local authorities were, on the whole, against a separate department for universities and related bodies, while the universities themselves, for the most part, looked upon the creation of a separate department as essential for the preservation of their interests. The government's response was in a sense a compromise because although relations with the universities, still through the agency of the University Grants Committee, were transferred from the Treasury to the Ministry of Education the latter department, under the new title of Department of Education and Science, became in effect a "federal" ministry, with a schools and further education "side" and a universities and civil science "side" (for some months each side had its own permanent secretary). Subsequently government support for the arts was also transferred from the Treasury so the Department of Education and Science resembles an amalgam between the former Ministry of Education and the Robbins ministry of the arts and sciences. It is significant that the organisational structure of the department places universities in a different category from the higher technical colleges, which are dealt with along with the schools side. A further anomaly is that the department is responsible for the Scottish universities, although the schools and further education system in Scotland come under the Secretary of State for Scotland. It is impossible to discover in this complex organisational pattern any clear concept of function and it is not surprising that the argument has been advanced that universities and civil science have closer affinities with the applied science responsibilities of the Ministry of Technology than with the other responsibilities of the Department of Education and Science. Such a reorganisation, it was claimed, would acknowledge the close link between universities and research, particularly scientific research (applied, as well as "pure") on which the Robbins Committee had placed such emphasis.

Science and Technology

The whole development of government organisation for science and technology since the First World War—the first major step, the creation of the Department of Scientific and Industrial Research, was taken in 1916—provides another admirable example of the limitations of the simple functional principle in illuminating the problems of allocating departmental functions. In its complex heterogeneity the organisation almost defies logical analysis.

The encouragement and pursuit of scientific research, unlike most other governmental functions, was not a field in which government began as a predominant influence. Scientific research, mainly of a "pure" nature, already took place in autonomous universities and research institutes, while industry itself undertook research with more immediate application to industrial needs. But with the greater government involvement in national economic and industrial policy, and the increasing recognition of the vital necessity for national economic progress of scientific research—much of it falling outside the scope of existing private bodies and much of it, also, extremely costly to finance—government came to play a greater part in scientific activity.

Government participation in science may take several forms. In some fields—defence is an obvious example—it will be a major user and government departments may engage directly in scientific research. In others it will sponsor research in autonomous institutions because the research is considered of national importance and cannot be adequately financed from non-governmental sources. In yet others there will be no suitable existing agency to undertake research on a subject considered of national importance and the government may set up a special agency (e.g., Agricultural Research Council, Road Research Laboratory).

Immediately organisational problems present themselves. Where the government directly engages in research, should this be supervised by a single department of research or by the department whose major function is most closely analogous (e.g., medical research by the Ministry of Health, agricultural research by the Ministry of Agriculture)? Where the government is sponsoring research elsewhere, what should be the organisational framework to ensure some public accountability? And, in both cases, how can the creative freedom of the individual researcher be reconciled with some form of governmental supervision?

On the first question the Haldane Report of 1918 seemed to favour a compromise, with a department of research which would not, however, monopolise governmental scientific activities since individual departments might still have their own scientific sections. This was roughly the course followed down to 1964. The Lord President of the Council (from 1959, the Minister for Science) acted as the general supervising minister of government civil science (defence research coming under the defence departments and the Ministry of Supply, later Aviation), while individual departments also directly undertook appropriate scientific activity or sponsored it elsewhere.

The role of the Lord President as science co-ordinator arose from the rather curious organisational device adopted for government supervision of its agencies for scientific research and for sponsorship of research. It was felt that the ordinary departmental model would not be appropriate for the supervision of government scientists and even less so for that of scientists undertaking sponsored research in universities and other autonomous research institutes. Too rigid departmental control would be likely to affect adversely the quality of research (the 1957 "Sputnik" success of rigidly controlled Soviet science was still in the future). Thus instead of coming under a single departmental minister activities like those of the Department of Scientific and Industrial Research (1916), Medical Research Council (1920), and Agricultural Research Council (1931) were nominally directed by a committee of the Privy Council under the chairmanship of the Lord President and with a membership of ministers departmentally concerned (in the case of the M.R.C., for example, the Secretaries of State for the Home Department, Scotland, Commonwealth Relations and the Colonies, and the Ministers of Health and Labour). In practice the committees rarely met and the operative member in each case was the Lord President, assisted by a small office. The creation of a non-departmental Minister for Science in 1959 affected this but little, since from 1960 to 1964 he was also Lord President.

In 1962 an official committee (under Sir Burke Trend, the Secretary to the Cabinet) was established to examine the functions and financing of government organisation for civil science. Its report, published in October 1963, recognised that special considerations arose in governmental relations with science since the responsible minister had to encourage conditions in which research could flourish without seeking to supervise the scientific judgement of the research agencies. But, not surprisingly, the committee was critical of existing arrangements. A system whereby responsibility for civil scientific research was fragmented and dispersed among a large number of agencies differing in status, scope, and autonomy was not, the committee felt, one which conduced to either the concentration or flexibility of effort which was becoming increasingly important in scientific research and development. Science was continually developing and expanding in new directions and government organisation for the promotion of scientific research "should be sufficiently precise and definite to provide a clear centre for co-ordination for each branch of research activity at any given moment and sufficiently flexible to ensure that new growing points of knowledge . . . are fostered". Both precision and flexibility, however, presupposed "a rational structure organically articulated".

It is difficult to believe that the reorganisation subsequently undertaken—much of it incorporated in the Science and Technology Act of 1965—has produced the Trend Committee's desideratum of "a rational structure organically articulated". The two principal general co-ordinating ministers are now the Secretary of State for Education and Science and the Minister of Technology. The Secretary of State, advised by the Council for Scientific Policy, is responsible for basic and applied civil science and for directing and financing the Science, Medical, Agricultural, Natural Environment, and Social Science Research Councils. The Minister of Technology, with the assistance of an Advisory Council on Technology, is responsible for promoting advanced technology and new processes in industry and for the activities of the United Kingdom Atomic Energy Authority, the National Research Development Council (an independent body set up in 1949 to secure the development and exploitation of inventions in the national interest), nine of the research establishments of the former Department of Scientific and Industrial Research (wound up in 1965), and seven defence research establishments of the former Ministry of Aviation (disbanded in 1967). Among the co-ordinating machinery is the Central Advisory Council on Science and Technology, under the Chief Scientific Adviser to the Government (who is in the Cabinet Office).

Other ministers have important responsibilities for scientific research. The Minister of Transport, for example, is responsible for the Road Research Laboratory, the Secretary of State for Defence for the Meteorological Office, the Minister of Public Building and Works for the Building Research Station, the Minister of Agriculture for veterinary laboratories, food research and research by the Forestry Commission, the Postmaster General for communications research, the Minister of Housing and Local Government for research on land use, and the Minister of Power for the oversight of research in the fuel and power and steel industries. Four ministers are principally involved in the government's space research programme—the Secretaries of State for Education and Science and for Defence, the Minister of Technology, and the Postmaster General.

Distribution of Responsibilities

External Relations

It was not until the merging of the Commonwealth Office with the Foreign Office in 1968 that Britain had a single department with the primary responsibility for the conduct of the country's external relations (the Treasury and Board of Trade continued, of course, to be concerned in overseas financial and trade policy). For a period of over forty years—since the separation of the Dominions Office from the Colonial Office in 1925—an administrative distinction had been made for the purposes of Britain's external relations between those countries which are independent members of the Commonwealth (together with the Irish Republic, even after it had left the Commonwealth in 1949—a precedent which was not followed when South Africa left the Commonwealth) and those which are not. On Haldane principles the existence of a department specifically to perform the function of supervising Britain's Commonwealth relationships could be seen as an example of the functional principle for allocating departmental responsibilities. But the actual operation of the Office revealed that complexity of the workings of government which tends to be under-estimated in attempts to establish "principles of administration". Looked at in one way, Commonwealth relations might constitute a major function, but in another—as the Commonwealth member countries are scattered over the globe—it is a regional or "place" responsibility. And in yet another aspect of its role the Commonwealth Office, as the voice of the Commonwealth in the Whitehall policy-formulating process, was a "clientele" department, acting as a kind of pressure group and focal point for the Commonwealth.

The division of responsibility between the Commonwealth and Foreign Offices clearly raised difficulties in the implementation of a coherent external relations policy—as, for example, in Cyprus and South-east Asia (the Indonesian-Malaysian "confrontation") in the 1960s—but this could be said to be counterbalanced by the special significance of the Commonwealth relationship. Increasingly, however, doubts came to be expressed as to the value of the Commonwealth association to Britain, especially as the expansion of its membership brought even greater diversity of aims and outlook. Britain alone among Commonwealth countries maintained a separate department for Commonwealth relations: elsewhere administrative recognition of the fact of the Commonwealth went no further than a special section within a general external ministry. Had the Commonwealth relationship become so attenuated that it no longer ranked a Whitehall department to itself? Was there still a Commonwealth relations function distinct from a general external relations function? Such questions increasingly came to be asked in the 1960s.

It was the Report of the Plowden Committee on Britain's overseas representational services in February 1964 which stimulated the most comprehensive discussion of a departmental merger. The committee's main conclusion was that "the division of the world, for representational purposes, into Commonwealth and non-Commonwealth countries impedes the development and execution of a coherent foreign policy"; and its principal recommendation, that the two overseas departments should draw their staff from a single, unified Diplomatic Service (this was established in 1965). The committee admitted that the "logic of events" pointed to a departmental amalgamation and recommended that this should be the ultimate aim. But it came to the conclusion that the moment was not yet opportune for a complete merger since it might be "misinterpreted as implying a loss of interest in the Commonwealth". Both the then Conservative government and its Labour successor accepted this judgement, for the moment. On the British side fears were expressed that a combined office would involve impossible burdens for its ministerial head, and lead to a muting of the Commonwealth's voice in the Whitehall "corridors of power". Four years later (1968) the full merger was announced, and little objection was raised, either in Britain or the overseas Commonwealth. It would seem reasonable to assume that the combined Foreign and Commonwealth Office could ensure adequate consideration of the Commonwealth viewpoint (or rather, viewpoints) in the formulation of British policy, backed by all those other channels, formal and informal, official and unofficial, British and overseas, for the expression of a Commonwealth consciousness. There was, however, a residual problem as a result of the earlier absorption of the Colonial Office by the Commonwealth Office (in 1966), namely, the administrative arrangements for the few remaining colonial territories for which independent nationhood was impracticable. Their supervision is not logically part of the external relations function and some felt that the Home Office would provide a more appropriate departmental *milieu* than the Foreign Office.

External relations can never, of course, be the monopoly of one department. One of the striking features of British administration, particularly since 1945, has been the way in which it has become internationalised, and few Whitehall departments are without overseas links of some kind. They include, as well as the obvious examples of the Treasury, the Board of Trade, the Ministry of Overseas Development (which, in addition to channelling aid, represents Britain in U.N.E.S.C.O. and F.A.O.), and the Ministry of Defence, the Department of Employment and Productivity, which represents Britain in I.L.O., and the Department of Health and Social Security, which represents Britain in W.H.O., and is concerned with pensioners living overseas. In fact at least a dozen home departments can be said to be "regularly involved in the activities of overseas representation and in policy decisions with extensive international applications" (D.C. Watt).

For Further Reading

Beer, S. H., *Treasury Control* (Oxford U.P., 2nd edn., 1957).
Beloff, Max, *New Dimensions in Foreign Policy* (Allen & Unwin, 1961).
Bridges, Lord, *The Treasury* (Allen & Unwin, 2nd edn., 1967).
Britain: An Official Handbook (H.M.S.O., annually).
Brittan, Samuel, *The Treasury under the Tories, 1951–1964* (Penguin Books, 1964).
Chester, D. N., and Willson, F. M. G., *The Organisation of British Central Government 1914–1964* (Allen & Unwin, 1968).
Cross, J. A., "The Beginning and End of the Commonwealth Office" in *Public Administration*, 47 (1969), 113–19.
Cross, J. A., *Whitehall and the Commonwealth: British Departmental Organisation for Commonwealth Relations 1900–1966* (Routledge & Kegan Paul, 1967).

"Fulton Report"—*Report of the Committee on the Civil Service 1966–68* (Cmnd. 3638, H.M.S.O., 1968). Chapter 7.

Grove, J. W., *Government and Industry in Britain* (Longmans, 1962).

Gulick, Luther, "Notes on the Theory of Organizations" in Gulick and Urwick, L. F. (eds.), *Papers on the Science of Administration* (Institute of Public Administration, New York, 1937).

"Haldane Report"—*Report of the Machinery of Government Committee* (Cmnd. 9230, H.M.S.O., 1918).

Mackenzie, W. J. M., "The Structure of Central Administration" in Campion, Sir Gilbert (*et al.*), *British Government since 1918* (Allen & Unwin, 1950).

Mackenzie, W. J. M., and Grove, J. W., *Central Administration in Britain* (Longmans, 1957).

"Plowden Report" (1)—*Report of the Committee on the Control of Public Expenditure*, (Cmnd. 1432, H.M.S.O., 1961).

"Plowden Report" (2)—*Report of the Committee on Representational Services Overseas*, (Cmnd. 2276, H.M.S.O., 1964).

"Robbins Report"—*Report of the Committee on Higher Education* (Cmnd. 2154, H.M.S.O., 1963).

Roll, Sir Eric (*et al.*), "The Machinery for Economic Planning" in *Public Administration*, 44 (1966), 1–72.

"Trend Report"—*Report of the Committee of Inquiry into the Organisation of Civil Science* (Cmnd. 2171, H.M.S.O., 1963).

Watt, D. C., "The Home Civil Service and the New Diplomacy" in *Political Quarterly*, 38 (1967), 283–9.

Whitehall and Beyond (B.B.C. Publications, 1964).

4. Government Departments: Co-ordination and Internal Organisation

However precise the distribution of responsibilities between government departments—and, as we have seen, the Whitehall pattern is in fact not conspicuous for its precision—it can never remove the overlapping of functions and the consequent necessity to secure co-ordination between different parts of the administrative machine. A relatively humble example—that of civil defence—will perhaps illustrate the universality of this process better than the more major aspects of government policy, such as defence, external relations and economic affairs, where the need for co-ordinating machinery of some kind is obvious. Although the Home Secretary and, in Scotland, the Secretary of State for Scotland, are responsible for civil defence functions under the Civil Defence Act of 1948, at least six other departments—the Ministries of Agriculture, Housing and Local Government, Power and Transport, the Department of Health and Social Security and the Welsh Office—have civil defence duties designated by order-in-council.

At the ministerial level there is the Cabinet and its committee system which has been described in Chapter 2. At the official level the almost ubiquitous device is the interdepartmental committee, usually chaired by an official of the department most directly concerned and with a membership from all the other departments affected. The device is not a supra-departmental one, however, for departmental autonomy is insisted upon even, in theory, to the extent of taking obdurate inter-departmental conflict to the Cabinet itself. In most cases, of course, the matter can be settled at a lower, official level, and officials will normally pride themselves on their ability to prevent inter-departmental issues from getting to the point when they have to "go to ministers".

Then there are explicitly co-ordinating ministries, as the Ministry of Defence was in the services field from 1946 to 1964, and as the Department of Economic Affairs, to a lesser extent, has been in the co-ordination of economic policy since its creation in 1964 and as the new Civil Service Department is intended to be in the personnel field. Such co-ordinating functions are also exercised principally through the agency of inter-departmental committees, in which the co-ordinating ministry may have rather more influence than the sponsoring department in a normal inter-departmental committee, by virtue of its specific co-ordinating role.

Treasury Control

The major co-ordinating department is the Treasury which, unlike the Department of Economic Affairs, can back its own influence with obvious sanctions—its control over the expenditure of every government department. In part, it is a parliamentary responsibility, both in form—for example, the Commons Public Accounts Committee laid it down in 1861 that the estimates of departmental expenditure must be approved by the Treasury before they are presented to Parliament—and in practice, since the Commons looks to the Treasury for the detailed check that it is incapable of doing itself. The scope of Treasury control over expenditure is difficult to define and, rather surprisingly, the definitions attempted in Treasury minutes of 1868 and 1914 are still considered formally applicable in the very different circumstances of today. A more recent description of current practice by the Treasury (in a memorandum to the Select

Committee on Estimates in 1958) records that "Treasury approval is necessary for every item of new expenditure, for any new service, or for any change of policy which involves an increase in expenditure, subject to any delegated authority which may have been given to particular departments in particular fields of expenditure". In addition the Treasury can intervene to question the scale or continuance of expenditure which does not require specific approval, or which has previously received approval, and this the Treasury does in its annual scrutiny of departmental estimates before their presentation to Parliament in February. It is recognised, however, that estimates embody departmental policy and it is symbolic that each permanent secretary—the chief official responsible for advising the minister on policy—has since 1920 formally been designated as the departmental accounting officer. The knotty problem of departmental autonomy obviously arises here and elaborate conventions have been developed in the intimate and continuous relationship between the Treasury and the spending departments. Within the over-riding responsibility of the Treasury to match total expenditure and total resources, the responsibility of the departments in financial matters and the impracticability in modern conditions of the Treasury vetting every item of expenditure is recognised in the practice of delegating financial authority to the individual department. The determination of the degree of such delegation depends upon striking a balance between, on the one hand, swamping the Treasury in detail and duplicating the financial scrutiny of the department itself and, on the other, giving the Treasury sufficient evidence of the kind of work being done to enable it to evaluate the department's own control. As the Treasury's 1958 memorandum put it: "The business of Treasury control is, in essence, the exercise by laymen of judgement upon the proposals of experts. It is no part of the Treasury business to attempt to rival the departments in the expert knowledge which they possess in their own field. What is necessary is to test the projects put forward and to obtain enough information to form a judgement as to whether the schemes are well founded; to make sure that enthusiasm does not run ahead

of prudence and commonsense, and to bear in mind the
remark of the Haldane Committee that 'our whole experience
seems to show that the interests of the taxpayer cannot be left
to the spending departments'."

As regards departmental policy Treasury control of
expenditure is essentially negative rather than positive,
critical rather than creative, and the department remains in a
real sense responsible for its own policy. In any case a final
court of appeal is available in the Cabinet in cases of intransi-
gent confrontation between Treasury and department, and
the Treasury—in a somewhat isolated position in a Cabinet
principally composed of the heads of spending departments—by no means always wins. The disadvantage of this
kind of arbitration, however—and it is true of a wide range
of governmental decision-making—is that (as the 1961
Plowden Report on the control of public expenditure put it)
"Discussion among ministers is likely to centre on the merits
of the particular proposal in relation at most to a general
background of the financial situation, rather than upon the
competing claims on the present and future resources of the
country which are represented by the aggregate of the spending
policies of the government". Hence the Plowden Committee,
and others, have recommended that decisions involving
substantial future expenditure should always be taken in the
light of surveys (by the Treasury) of public expenditure as a
whole, over a period of years, and in relation to the prospective resources. The Treasury is no doubt trying to implement this recommendation (the method was described in a
1966 White Paper), and its 1962 reorganisation was in part
intended to assist it to do so, but it is clearly an undertaking
which depends upon a general economic stability which is not
easily secured.

It must be said that on the whole the Treasury is scrupulous—some think too scrupulous—in respecting departmental
autonomy. Indeed the implication of recommendations by
informed observers—as with the Select Committee on Estimates in 1958 and the Plowden Committee to which it gave
rise—is often that the Treasury should intervene more effectively in the working of individual departments in order to

ensure overall consistency and efficiency. It is here that Treasury control over establishments played an important part since in a sense it is a more direct influence even than scrutiny of expenditure as it concerned personnel and office methods. The Plowden Report put particular emphasis on the Treasury responsibility, *inter alia*, "for the overall efficiency of the public service, and thus for seeing that the departments are staffed, particularly at the top levels, with the best available officers drawn from the service as a whole" and "for the development of management services throughout the public service; for taking the initiative in the introduction of new management techniques; and for keeping an oversight over the management practice of all the departments".

Treasury control of establishments formally dated from 1868 when a Treasury minute made Treasury sanction a prerequisite for any increase in staff numbers. In 1919 the Permanent Secretary of the Treasury was designated official Head of the Civil Service (later changed to *Home* Civil Service, thus excluding the Diplomatic Service), and in the following year an order-in-council empowered the Treasury to "make regulations for controlling the conduct of His Majesty's Civil Establishments, and providing for the classification, remuneration and other conditions of service of all persons employed therein, whether permanently or temporarily". All senior appointments—permanent secretaries, deputy secretaries, and principal finance and establishments officers—were to be made by the Prime Minister in consultation with the Head of the Civil Service.

The increase in size of the Civil Service resulting from the Second World War and its aftermath made the full rigours of the old system impracticable and, following a review in 1949, the major departments (in this context those whose establishment officer was of under-secretary rank) were given considerable freedom to control their own numbers—up to 90 per cent or more—within a ceiling negotiated with the Treasury; only new senior posts and staff expenditure on any new or greatly expanded function required specific Treasury approval. The Plowden Committee's emphasis on good management led, in the 1962 reorganisation, to the abolition of the old "mixed" Treasury divisions which dealt with both expenditure and establishments of the same departments and the substitution of a more functional organisation. Thus the Treasury "side" under the Head of the Home Civil Service now differentiated organisationally between *personnel recruitment policy* (the actual selection of individuals being left to the independent Civil Service Commission); *career management*, including training (although much of the training, especially at the lower levels, is done in the departments); and *management services*, including Organisation and Methods (for which the Treasury acts as a central clearing house of information, providing O. & M. services for departments without O. & M. divisions of their own, and training O. & M. staff), office machines (e.g., automatic data processing), machinery of government questions, comparative studies (in industry and overseas), and costing techniques.

Following the 1968 recommendations of the Fulton Report (already discussed in this context in Chapter 3, see above, p. 47), the pay and management side of the Treasury—together with the Civil Service Commission—have been absorbed by the new Civil Service Department. The Prime Minister, assisted by another Cabinet minister, supervises the department, whose permanent head is the Head of the Home Civil Service. The Fulton Committee, in line with its general recommendations for Civil Service reform (see below, p. 79), envisaged the new department playing a more positive part than had the Treasury in the central management of the Civil Service. The guiding principle should, the committee felt, be the delegation to individual departments of the maximum authority in staff and organisation matter compatible with the requirements of the Service as a whole. On questions of departmental efficiency and organisation the main role of the central department should be to encourage the use of the most modern techniques; it may have a special function to perform in assisting reorganisation at the higher levels of departments; and it should, in the last resort, be in a position to call departments to account if they fail to use the recommended techniques (the committee did not specify how this sanction would operate in practice), to carry out investigations of departmental organisation and to recommend improvements. In the management of staff, especially the planning of careers, the committee thought that the main responsibility must remain with the individual departments, but that the central department should play a larger part, and have more ultimate authority, than had the Treasury. It should be responsible for informing itself about those civil servants who are identified as capable of filling highest posts, should consult with the employing departments about their training and development, and should take the initiative in proposing appropriate moves. It should have a voice in promotions of senior staff and be represented on the appropriate departmental promotion boards.

Internal Organisation and the Civil Service

The internal pattern of government departments stems essentially from the Civil Service reforms of the second half of the nineteenth century (the Northcote-Trevelyan Report, as implemented by the order-in-council of 1870) which substituted a unified permanent career Civil Service, divided into classes with specific functions for the most part considered applicable to every government department, for a series of more or less separate departmental staffs recruited mainly by ministerial patronage. The reforms thus symbolised the marriage of responsible government—in the shape of lay, temporary ministers accountable for their departments to the public and Parliament—and administrative expertise, corporately possessed by the hierarchy of permanent officials in each department. The main chain of command ran from the minister through the small administrative class (as it came to be known) which was primarily concerned with assisting the minister with the conduct of parliamentary business, the preparation of legislation, departmental finance, and the general oversight of the department's work. The larger executive class was responsible for regulatory and supervisory work within the framework of existing departmental policy, while the larger clerical class was charged with the more routine office business. Most departments had legal staffs from an early stage and recruitment of other specialist staffs—medical officers, scientists, economists, information officers and so on—gradually extended. But the traditional supremacy of the administrative class and their special relation to the minister remained—the specialists were (in the familiar phrase) on tap rather than on top.

The actual organisation of each department's work exhibits the same kind of principles as are considered in the distribution of functions between departments. Some departmental divisions are reproduced in most departments—such as establishments and organisation, finance, legal, and information—while others reflect the special nature of the department's work. Thus departments dealing with overseas affairs are organised on a geographical as well as on a subject or functional basis, while departments concerned primarily with home affairs are mainly organised functionally. Some departments, especially those concerned with social services, have regional organisations (which will be examined in Chapter 5). All are organised hierarchically—fundamental to any bureaucratic organisation—with a permanent secretary supervising the whole department and sharing with one or more deputy secretaries the oversight of particular blocks of the department's work, organised in divisions, branches and offices (to use generic rather than specific terms since terminology varies from department to department) under under-secretaries, assistant secretaries, and principals or their executive or specialist class analogues (in the case, for example, of an accounts division or a legal division).

This traditional pattern still remains in essence but has not been unaffected by the increasing complexity and specialisation of governmental business—by the fact that in each department "More decisions have to be made, more information assembled, more expert enquiries put in hand, more interested bodies consulted" (P. Self). The changes may be conveniently examined in the context of three sets of relationships—those between the minister and his senior officials, between general administrators and specialists, and between departments and their "organised publics". The process of change is now fundamentally affected by the governmental acceptance of the main recommendations of the Fulton Report, which is summarised at the end of this chapter.

When departments were small and their functions relatively routine and non-technical it was possible for ministers who had the desire and ability to dominate their work, as did Joseph Chamberlain that of the Colonial Office from 1895 to 1903 or Haldane that of the War Office from 1905 to 1912. The role of the senior official was to "encourage advise and warn" and, once the minister had made his decision, to implement it loyally and efficiently. This is still essentially the case but the growing range and complexity of the average department's work has necessarily had its effect. The minister can see only a fraction of the matters which come up for decision in the department (although his officials will devote themselves to ensuring that all those with important political implications do so) and in most cases the considerations will be so complex that the minister will have to rely almost entirely upon departmental briefing, normally channelled through the permanent secretary. This clearly raises the possibility of the minister's decision being influenced not so much by the intrinsic merits (in so far as these can be judged) but by the way in which his officials have presented the alternatives. Wedgwood Benn, for example, has described how, after he had become Postmaster General in 1964, he found that although he could veto proposals he could initiate hardly any of his own. He was not expected to meet any but the most senior staff in the department, and papers reached him in neat summary form, requiring only an affirmative or a negative answer (*Sunday Times*, 20th February, 1966). Benn's Conservative predecessor at the Post Office, Reginald Bevins, has also graphically described the difficulties in the path of a minister contemplating the introduction of major changes in departmental policy. Peter Shore—himself subsequently a Cabinet minister—has written of a "dangerously unbalanced and dependent" relationship of ministers with their civil servants, while the Labour Party submission to the Fulton Committee on the Civil Service referred to some ministers being "tools of their departments a good deal of the time" since "it is impossible for a minister to have an adequate grasp of an issue if he plays no part in the long process of discussion which precedes the formation of policy". Others have made a similar point without drawing the same conclusion. An academic summing-up of a discussion of the question to which a former Cabinet minister (Sir Edward Boyle) and a former permanent secretary (Sir Edward Playfair) had contributed, recognised that ministers are presented with options from which they must attempt to select—that officials dominate the "fact-finding, analysis and recommendations" side of policy-making—but argued that ministers still effectively have the last word on the bulk of important issues.

Those who feel that in modern circumstances a minister, however able, is in some sense a "tool of his department" have recommended the introduction into British departmental practice of something akin to the French ministerial "Cabinet" system whereby a minister brings with him into his department on appointment a group of personally-selected political and expert advisers owing their first loyalty to him and sieving for him the material coming up from the established hierarchy. Thus the Labour Party evidence to the Fulton Committee proposed that a minister should have the right to appoint a limited number of personal assistants, perhaps up to four, with direct access to him and to all the information in the department. They would take no administrative decisions themselves but "act as a political brains trust to the minister".

Recommendations like this would seem to rest on the assumption that the minister is in a sense engaged in isolated dialogues with his senior officials. Such isolation, if it exists, can only be true of the minister *within* his own department. In the machinery of ministerial co-ordination—in Cabinet and Cabinet committee—the minister must argue his departmental case with his ministerial colleagues, for the most part unassisted by his officials, who must obviously accept a decision of a higher authority (officials are, indeed, anxious for their minister to perform well in inter-ministerial discussions and here inclusion or exclusion from full membership of the Cabinet is almost as important to the department as to the minister himself). But how far is a minister in fact isolated within his department?

There is, in general, nothing to prevent ministers bringing outside advisers into their departments on a temporary basis, and this has been increasingly done since 1964, particularly in the newer departments like the Department of Economic Affairs and the Ministry of Technology. But over and above this inevitably rather small-scale process (since a large importation of outsiders would be likely to have serious effects on the concept of a permanent service and on Civil Service morale) there are two institutions which modify the minister's isolation in his department—one long-established, the other a more recent development. The first is the minister's "Private Office", consisting of his Civil Service secretary (a principal or assistant secretary) and assistant secretaries, together with the M.P. who acts in the unofficial and unpaid capacity of parliamentary private secretary to the minister. The Civil Service secretaries are the minister's main "eyes and ears" in the department and have to combine a loyalty to the minister with a loyalty to the department in which their careers are based. They normally maintain the balance with discretion and delicacy but the dual allegiance necessarily affects their relationship with the minister. The P.P.S. can be more single-mindedly devoted to his minister's interests but his influence in the department is naturally limited (although some ministers make a practice of discussing major political issues with their P.P.S.).

A newer development is the appearance of ministerial "teams" at the head of departments. The pattern was for long one of a minister assisted by one junior minister (parliamentary secretary), with whom his relations might not be particularly close (especially if, as often happened, the junior minister was appointed by the Prime Minister without reference to the departmental minister concerned). But with the increasing use of the intermediate post of minister of state and the appointment of more than one parliamentary secretary to several departments few departmental heads are now assisted by only one junior ministerial colleague. Of nineteen ministerial departments at the beginning of 1969 only four had the minimum provision while twelve departments had three or more ministers in addition to the departmental head. Under the overall supervision of the minister (who retains his formal accountability to Parliament) the work of the department is often divided up in a quite formal way between the subordinate ministers, who thus provide a further political check on recommendations coming from the officials. This is particularly the case where ministries have been merged with others (e.g., the Ministry of Land and Natural Resources with the Ministry of Housing and Local Government and the Ministry of Aviation with the Ministry of Technology) and a full minister or a minister of state continues to have special responsibility for the merged functions. It may be that ministers do not always make full use of their junior colleagues—in the Foreign Office, for example, the institution by George Brown of weekly meetings of the five Foreign Office ministers on his appointment as Foreign Secretary in 1966 was considered somewhat revolutionary (*Sunday Times*, 7th April, 1968)—but it renders less inevitable the minister's isolation in his contacts with his officials and properly used might well modify the need for a ministerial Cabinet or brains trust.

But what of the officials themselves and the relationship between the various categories of officials? Civil Service recruitment, following Northcote-Trevelyan precepts, has traditionally emphasised the securing of general ability, at various levels of the educational system, which can then be trained "on the job" to carry out the necessary tasks efficiently. Thus the 2,500 strong administrative class, mainly drawn from the best university graduates, is (to quote an official text) responsible for advising ministers on policy, for dealing with any difficulties which may arise in carrying out official policy, for forecasting the probable effects of new measures and regulations, and, in general, for the broad problems which arise in the running of the government machine. The executive class (now with over 80,000 members), originally recruited mainly from sixth formers, is responsible for the day-to-day conduct of government business within the framework of established policy (for example, departmental accounts and personnel matters). The considerably larger clerical class (over 190,000) is concerned with the more routine operations and, unlike the executive class, does not have a hierarchy of grades (the most senior executive class officials rank with under-secretaries in the administrative class). The assumption behind such classification is that there is a common element running through the work of each government department—however disparate and technical their functions—which can be performed by any member of the appropriate general Civil Service class. For the clerical class and all but the highest grades of the executive class this seems a reasonable assumption, but the case is not so clear with the policy advice and formulation role of the administrative class.

At one time—especially in the inter-war years—criticism of recruitment methods for the administrative class (there has been little criticism of those for the other classes) centred on the restricted group—predominantly Oxford and Cambridge graduates—from which it was drawn. This was thought to produce an upper middle class official, isolated from the life of ordinary people and little disposed to react positively to the stimulus of a reforming government, indeed, likely to obstruct, overtly or covertly, the policies of such a government. Such criticism is much less frequently made nowadays, partly because of actual experience since 1945 (of Labour governments on taking office in 1945 and 1964); partly because the social basis of " Oxbridge " students has completely changed since the war (and, in any case, the Oxbridge predominance among the young graduate entry is less than it was, the ratio now being about 3:2, compared with 4:1 a few years ago); and partly because of the now substantial "mature" entry into the administrative class. Mature entrants come either as a result of promotion from other classes (mainly the executive)—which accounts for a third of the whole class—or by direct entry from people with outside experience including, since 1964, some at assistant secretary level. A quarter of the members of the administrative class are not graduates, a most significant change from the pre-1939 pattern of recruitment. It may be added that even when the

Civil Service was in fact largely recruited from a restricted social class (as to some extent the equivalent of the administrative class within the Diplomatic Service still is) it remained open to doubt whether the introduction of explicit recruitment from wider social groups would have made the Civil Service more attentive to the needs of those groups.

An issue rather more relevant to the efficiency of public administration is the nature of the role which the administrative class feels called upon to play. Senior officials have looked upon themselves as advisers to ministers, as supervisors of the operation of the departmental machine, rather than as creative initiators of policy (which, perhaps understandably, they have conceived to be the primary function of ministers). The permanent secretary is thus a chief of staff rather than a managing director, senior officials advisers rather than commanders, "machine-minders" rather than "machine-designers". In part this is inevitable since assisting ministers in their parliamentary business is an essential task of senior officials. The question remains whether they should also be performing other tasks and whether they have the qualifications to perform them.

One of the main tasks which needs to be discharged is managerial, involving both management of personnel—most departments are in fact large-scale organisations—and policy planning. The Fulton Report, which placed emphasis on this aspect of the civil servant's role, defined management as responsibility for "organisation, directing staff, planning the progress of work, setting standards of achievement and measuring results, reviewing procedures and quantifying different courses of action". The personnel management function in departments (under general Treasury supervision) has been traditionally associated with the executive class, something with which the administrative class is not normally concerned. On the industrial analogy—and here it seems most appropriate—this is a curious down-grading of an important function, though the Treasury proposal to the Fulton Committee that the administrative and executive classes should be merged at the higher levels was clearly designed, among other things, to redress the balance here.

Co-ordination and Internal Organisation

Deficiences in departmental forward planning—the informed anticipation of future needs and their organisational consequences—had been widely commented upon well before the publication of the Fulton Report. Remedies were sought in the secondment of officials for periods in industry (both private and nationalised) and local government and in a more intensive training in management techniques. Secondments have taken place to a limited extent but the problems of finding convenient niches in outside industry (where the work is obviously different from that of government departments) and of releasing officials from their posts—where they are not normally under-employed—seemed to militate against any large-scale introduction. Civil Service training, which was reviewed by the Assheton Committee in 1944, has remained somewhat spasmodic and *ad hoc*, but the establishment in 1963 of the Treasury's Centre for Administrative Studies—which, among other things, provides a twenty-eight week course for assistant principals in their third year of service in such subjects as economics, statistics, industry, trade unions, and the relation of government to science and technology—was an indication of a new approach.

A possible corollary of an increasing emphasis on the managerial role of civil servants, particularly the most senior officials, is their greater involvement in public discussion of policy questions, in a way which has long been characteristic of senior local government officials (e.g., chief education officers), who are in every sense managers as well as policy advisers. The staff association which represents the administrative class, in its submission to the Fulton Committee, indeed advocated the participation of civil servants in open discussion of policy alternatives confronting their departments. For long anonymity has been considered to be the main guarantee of Civil Service impartiality, making it possible to have a permanent Civil Service remaining in post to advise changing political administrations. But although abnegation of partisan political activity, in the sense of working for the achievement of, or continuation in, power by a particular political party, is an obvious necessity for senior civil servants (and is now enshrined in the procedures elaborated in 1953 on the basis of the 1949 Masterman Report on the political activities of civil servants) impartiality, in the sense of complete neutrality, of non-commitment to the policies of the government they are serving at any one time, has always seemed a rather artificial concept. Civil servants are already the main departmental points of contact for the multiplicity of interest groups with which the government has dealings and have to conduct often delicate negotiations with such bodies. An increasing number of civil servants are involved in international negotiations, too—for example, in the United Nations and its various agencies or in the attempts by Britain to secure entry into the European Economic Community—and can hardly avoid public identification with governmental policies. This will similarly be the case if it is generally accepted that senior civil servants are managers and initiators as well as policy advisers and increasingly contribute as such to public discussions. The possibility then arises of circumstances in which a change of government, even merely a change of minister, might lead to embarrassment if a senior official has been too closely associated in public with a policy which is to be discarded or fundamentally revised. There is then the question (discussed in the Fulton Report, see below, p. 85) of how far the removal of such an official is compatible with the preservation of the party political neutrality of the Service.

A problem connected with that of the civil servant as manager as well as administrator is the familiar one—not, of course, confined to government departments—of the relationship of "generalist" administrators to "specialist" or professional advisers, in other words, of "line and staff". The tradition has been that specialist advice within the department—from scientists, economists, medical officers, and so on—has been called for by, and transmitted through, the administrative hierarchy which, by the nature of its recruitment and its departmental tasks, is non-specialist; only rarely has it come through the specialist hierarchy itself culminating, for example, in a chief scientific adviser having direct access to the minister. This has been perhaps as much due to the personal proclivities of a usually non-technical minister (more at home in discussing the implications of

76

specialist advice with his generalist officials) than of the
obstinacy of the administrative class; non-specialist administrators are possibly less likely than experts to present their
views to ministers in the form of demands or to oppose the
minister's own plans (direct confrontation with technical
experts could conceivably increase the ministerial "isolation"
discussed earlier). But in consequence specialists have often
felt that their advice has been distorted in the process of lay
administrators attempting to interpret it to the minister;
that it has in any case only been asked for at the initiative
of the administrators; that they (the specialists) have little
chance to deploy their arguments again if their advice is
rejected; and that administrators are liable to re-apply the
advice in what they consider to be analogous circumstances
without re-consulting the specialists. The answer (at least
before the government's acceptance of the Fulton recommendation that Civil Service classes should be abolished)
seemed to lie either in transferring specialist officers more
readily to the administrative class (it is a common tendency
for the work of specialists themselves to become more administrative in nature the more senior they are) or in making the
organisational relationship between administrators and specialists in departments more articulated. Promotions from the
specialist classes to the administrative class have taken place
but one problem is the loyalty of a specialist to his professional
milieu, which often makes him reluctant to transfer. The
alternative approach of "interleaving" general administrators and specialists has been developed, particularly in
departments with work of a high technical content: separate
hierarchies of administrators and specialists have been replaced by parallel hierarchies or, in some cases joint or
integrated hierarchies. Thus since 1949 the Department of
Education and Science (or Ministry of Education as it was
then known) has had an architects and building branch headed
jointly by a chief architect and an under secretary and the
branch's development work has nearly always been undertaken by small *ad hoc* mixed professional and administrative
teams. In the Ministry of Public Building and Works two
parallel hierarchies were developed, operating throughout the

department, for the administrative side and for the research, development and production side, with the permanent secretary matched by a controller-general, deputy secretaries by directors-general and under secretaries by directors. The administrative (and, in some cases, executive) and professional officials were given joint responsibility for particular areas of the department's work but have carefully assigned and separate functions within their joint responsibility. (In 1969 the same ministry became the first government department to implement the fully integrated organisation recommended by the Fulton Committee.) The highways organisation of the Ministry of Transport—one of the three main groups into which the department is divided—is under a professional director-general (the other two groups are under deputy secretaries), below whom there are some divisions with joint administrative and specialist heads and some with single heads, either administrative or specialist. There is a similarly integrated organisation in the Ministry of Technology. This kind of arrangement is not necessarily appropriate for departments or sections within departments which are either, at one end of the scale, almost completely non-technical or, at the other, overwhelmingly technical. Thus even within the Ministry of Transport the administrative content of the bridges engineering group is too small and that of the finance and establishments divisions too great to warrant the integration of administrative and specialist staff within them.

The specialist-general administrator relationship is linked with the third set of changing departmental relationships referred to earlier—that of the department with the interest groups working in the field of its responsibilities. The more government has expanded the area of its operations the more groups of producers, professional workers, technical interests, and the like have organised themselves to influence governmental policy in their direction, either negatively or positively (they thus constitute a form of administrative control and are discussed as such in Chapter 8). Few government departments are without intimate links with appropriate interest groups, like that of the Ministry of Agriculture with the National Farmers Union or the Department of Education and Science with teachers' organisations, the Association of Education Committees, and other education bodies. A significant feature of British public administration has been the way in which these groups have been integrated in the machinery of government. *Ad hoc* committees on particular subjects, either royal commissions or departmental committees, with representation from appropriate interests, have been a long-standing device to assist the government as a whole or a particular department in the formulation of a policy (or, as it has been argued, sometimes to postpone the necessity of coming to policy decisions on some controversial topic). A more recent and now widespread technique has been that of *standing* advisory committees of interest group representatives, like the central advisory councils on education (for England and for Wales) attached to the Department of Education and Science, and the Central Health Services Advisory Committee which advises the Secretary of State for Social Services. The number of these committees runs into hundreds, the latest official computation, made in 1965, being 251; over three-quarters of them accounted for by only eight departments—the Scottish Office, the Ministry of Labour (as it then was), the Ministry of Agriculture, the Home Office, the Ministry of Public Building and Works, the Department of Education and Science, the Board of Trade, and the Ministry of Health (then a separate department). It could be colourably argued that the committees provide departments with the necessary expertise which the administrative officials are said to lack. But the crucial point is that, for the most part, this advisory machinery is activated only if the department takes the initiative (and in fact many of the committees meet very infrequently), and a body with an external membership must necessarily be on the fringes of policy-making, as opposed to a specialist official participating in the whole range of relevant departmental discussions.

The Fulton Report

The internal organisation of departments and the structure of the Civil Service which mans them have been fundamentally affected by the Fulton Report of 1968 and the government's acceptance of its main recommendations—although it will be several years before they are fully operative. The committee reported that it found the Civil Service inadequate for "the most efficient discharge of the present and prospective responsibilities of government" in six main respects:

(1) It is essentially based on "the philosophy of the amateur", most evident in the dominant position of the administrative class. The ideal administrator is seen as the gifted layman who, moving frequently from job to job in the Service, can take a practical view of any problem, irrespective of its subject matter, in the light of his knowledge and experience of the government machine. (A Treasury memorandum to the Select Committee on Estimates in 1964 showed that *all* the permanent secretaries then in post and three-quarters of the deputy secretaries had served in more than one department, while half the under secretaries and two-fifths of the assistant secretaries had also done so. Although only a fifth of the principals had served in more than one department they, like their seniors, were always liable to frequent moves to different jobs within the same department.)

(2) The present system of classes (forty-seven general classes and over 1,400 departmental classes) seriously impedes the Service's work. Each civil servant is recruited to a particular class and his membership of that class determines his career prospects and the range of jobs on which he may be employed; subsequent movement between classes is only a limited palliative. This compartmentalism hampers the Service in adapting itself to new tasks, prevents the best use of individual talent, contributes to the inequality of promotion prospects, causes frustration and resentment, and impedes the entry into wider management of those well fitted for it.

(3) Many scientists, engineers, and other specialists get neither the responsibilities nor the opportunities they ought to have. Too often they are organised in a separate hierarchy, while policy and financial aspects of the work are reserved to a parallel group of generalist administrators. In the new

Civil Service a wider and more important role must be opened up for specialists trained and equipped for it.

(4) Too few civil servants are skilled managers. One reason is that they are not adequately trained in management. Another is that much of their present work is not managerial in the sense the committee defined it (i.e., "organisation, directing staff, planning the progress of work, setting standards of achievement and measuring results, reviewing procedures and quantifying courses of action") and so administrative civil servants tend to think of themselves as advisers on policy to people above them rather than as managers of the administrative machine below them.

(5) There is not enough contact between the Civil Service and the rest of the community and consequently insufficient awareness in the Service of how the world outside Whitehall works, how government policies will affect it, and what new ideas and methods are being developed elsewhere.

(6) Career-planning is defective: civil servants are moved too frequently between unrelated jobs, often with little regard to personal preference or aptitude. There is not enough encouragement and reward for individual initiative and objectively measured performance; for many civil servants, especially in the lower grades, promotion depends too much on seniority.

From this diagnosis (which many considered under-estimated the extent of the changes already made or in train) the Fulton Committee proceeded to prescribe a cure. The proposal to establish a Civil Service Department has already been mentioned (see above, p. 47). Other important elements in the committee's prescription included the following:

(1) The separate classes should be abolished and replaced by a single grading structure in which there are an appropriate number of different pay-levels matching different levels of skill and responsibility, with the correct grading for each post determined by job evaluation. This unified grading structure would remove obstacles to flexible deployment of staff and enable the Service to gain the full contribution which scientists, engineers, and other specialist staff could make to

policy, management, and administration. It would also provide a more flexible career structure for administrative staff (including members of both the present administrative and executive classes) by enabling the Service to deploy them to the best advantage without transferring them from the executive class to the administrative class or *vice versa*.

(2) The Civil Service should develop greater professionalism among both specialists and administrators. For the former this means more training in management and opportunities for greater responsibilities and wider careers. For the latter it means enabling them to specialise in particular areas, either as economic and financial administrators or as social administrators. The economic and financial administrators should, in addition to administrative skills, have appropriate qualifications, experience, and training in such subjects as economics, finance, business administration, and statistics. They should be employed not only in the economic government departments but also in posts in any department that are mainly financial or concerned with economic administration and management. Social administrators should have training and experience in social studies relevant to modern government (e.g., social structure, regional planning, methods of social investigation, and the administration of social services) in addition to their administrative skills. While most social administrators would be concentrated in the main social departments they would, like their economic and financial counterparts, be employed throughout the Civil Service (e.g., in personnel work). Each department should have a suitable blend of administrators from both groups but they should not replace specialists in their departments (e.g., engineers, accountants, economists, sociologists), whose primary concern is the practice of their specialism. Thus the economic and financial administrators would not substitute for professional economists: they would not have the same depth of expertise and would be immersed in the day-to-day operations of the department in a way that would be inappropriate for the specialist economist. Similarly, a social administrator would not take the place of a specialist sociologist, for example. The aim is to produce a more fruitful

relationship than in the past between the administrator, trained and experienced in his subject-matter, and the specialist, and to harness the best contribution from each. And from these professional civil servants—administrators and specialists alike—would come the future top management of the Civil Service: experienced in running the government machine, expert in one or more aspects of the department's work, broadened by increasing responsibilities and experience to become the fully professional advisers of ministers, and managers of their policies.

(3) A Civil Service college should be set up to provide major training courses in administration and management and a wide range of shorter courses; it should also undertake research into problems of administration and the machinery of government and specific research projects commissioned by departments. The courses at the college should not be restricted to civil servants and a proportion of places should be set aside for men and women from private industrial and commercial firms, local government and public corporations.

(4) More resources should be devoted to the career management of all civil servants. All must have the opportunity to progress as far and as fast as their talents and appropriate training can take them. And while the Civil Service should remain predominantly a career service, there should be greater mobility between it and other employments. The committee therefore recommended an expanded appointment of late entrants with relevant experience, temporary appointments for fixed periods, short-term interchanges of staff, and freer movement out of the Service (e.g., by simplifying pension transfer arrangements).

(5) The principle of *accountable management* should be applied to the work of all departments, involving the clear allocation of responsibility and authority to accountable units with defined objectives. Where measures of achievement can be established in quantitative or financial terms (e.g., the payments of benefits or the handling of individual employment problems) and individuals held responsible for output and costs, accountable units should be set up. Work of this kind should be organised into separate "commands" under

managers with clear-cut responsibilities and commensurate authority and accountable for performance against budgets, standards of achievement, and other tests; within his unit each manager should set up sub-systems of responsibility and delegated authority.

In much administrative work, however, measurable output cannot always be made the criterion for assessing performance. It is not possible to lay down in advance, for example, how long it should take the responsible government department to review effectively the investment programme of a nationalised industry. Moreover such assessment is complicated by the unpredictable demands that arise from ministerial responsibility to Parliament and by the fact that much of the work contains a major element of new policy-making, involving consultation, negotiation, and the preparation of legislation. Thus the principle to be applied here is that of *management by objective*. Whether the branch is primarily concerned with administering existing policies, with planning new policies, or with research, its objectives and priorities need to be clearly established; individuals at all levels should know what they are responsible for and what authority they have. Each major government department should have a management services unit to undertake efficiency audits and promote the use of the best management techniques.

(6) To enable departments to undertake long-term policy-planning and research (frequently neglected in the past in the press of daily business in which most of the senior staff are engaged) a *planning and research unit* should be established in each department. Its main task would be to identify and study the problems and needs of the future and the possible means of meeting them; it should also see that day-to-day policy decisions are taken with as full a recognition as possible of their likely implications for the future. At its head should be a *senior policy adviser*, probably of deputy secretary rank, with direct and unrestricted access to the minister, as his chief adviser on the planning of longer-term departmental policy.

(7) The senior policy adviser, together with the permanent secretary and, in some big technical departments, a chief

scientist or chief engineer, should provide the official leadership of a department. The permanent secretary alone would continue, however, to have overall responsibility under the minister for all departmental affairs. The Fulton Committee saw no need for the introduction of ministerial "Cabinets" (see above, p. 70), nor for political appointments of ministerial advisers on a large scale, but it thought that a minister should be able to employ on a temporary basis such small numbers of experts as he personally considers he needs to advise him. The senior policy adviser might well come from outside the Civil Service—although he would more often be a career civil servant with long experience in, and expert knowledge of, the field covered by the department—but the committee hoped that a new minister would not normally wish to replace him. It recognised, however, that this must be possible when a new minister finds the current senior policy adviser too closely identified with, or wedded to, policies that he wishes to change; or when an adviser's capacity for producing and making use of new ideas declines. It should be more exceptional for a minister to change his permanent secretary. Any change of senior policy adviser or permanent secretary would require the most careful consideration by the Head of the Home Civil Service and the Prime Minister, whose joint task it is in this context to safeguard the political neutrality of the higher Civil Service. On the general question of the participation of civil servants in public discussion the committee was prepared to see the convention of anonymity modified to enable Civil Service administrators to play a greater part in explaining what their departments are doing, at any rate so far as concerns managing existing policies and implementing legislation.

In a statement on the Fulton Report in the House of Commons on 26th June, 1968, the Prime Minister announced the government's decision to accept the main recommendations of the report. He specifically mentioned the establishment of a new Civil Service Department (which began work in November 1968), within which specific and formal arrangements would be made to ensure the continued independence and political impartiality of the Civil Service Commission in the selection of individuals for appointment to the Civil Service; the Civil Service college; and the abolition of classes (but not professions) within the Service. Decisions on remaining recommendations would be announced at a later stage, following discussions with those concerned, particularly the Civil Service staff associations.

For Further Reading

Alderman, R. K., and Cross, J. A., "The Parliamentary Private Secretary" in *The Parliamentarian*, XLVIII (1967), 70–6.

Armstrong, Sir William (*et al.*), "The Fulton Report" in *Public Administration*, 47 (1969), 1–63.

Beer, S. H., *Treasury Control* (Oxford U.P., 2nd edn. 1957).

Bevins, Reginald, *The Greasy Pole* (Hodder & Stoughton, 1965).

Blondel, J., *Voters, Parties and Leaders* (Penguin Books, rev. edn., 1965).

Boyle, Sir Edward (*et al.*), "Who are the Policy Makers?" in *Public Administration* 43 (1965), 251–68, 281–7.

Bridges, Lord, *The Treasury* (Allen & Unwin, 2nd edn., 1967).

Britain: An Official Handbook (H.M.S.O., annually).

Brown, R. G. S., "Organization Theory and Civil Service Reform" in *Public Administration*, 43 (1965), 313–30.

Chapman, Brian, *British Government Observed* (Allen & Unwin, 1963).

Chapman, Brian, *The Profession of Government* (Allen & Unwin, 1959).

Chester, D. N. (*et al.*), "The Plowden Report" in *Public Administration*, 41 (1963), 1–50.

Dodd, C. H., and Pickering, J. F., "Recruitment to the Administrative Class, 1960–1964" in *Public Administration*, 45 (1967), 55–80, 169–99.

Dunnill, F., *The Civil Service: Some Human Aspects* (Allen & Unwin, 1956).

Finer, S. E., *Anonymous Empire: A Study of the Lobby in Great Britain* (Pall Mall, 2nd edn., 1965).

"Fulton Report"—Vol. 1: *Report of the Committee on the Civil Service 1966–68* (Cmnd. 3638, H.M.S.O., 1968).

"Fulton Report"—Vol. 2: *Report of a Management Consultancy Group* (H.M.S.O., 1968) (together with three other volumes of evidence).

Information and the Public Interest (Cmnd. 4089, H.M.S.O., 1969).

Keeling, C. D. E., "The Treasury Centre for Administrative Studies" in *Public Administration*, 43 (1965), 191–8.

Kelsall, R. K., *Higher Civil Servants in Britain* (Routledge & Kegan Paul, 1955).

"Masterman Report"—*Report of the Committee on the Political Activities of Civil Servants* (Cmnd. 7718, H.M.S.O., 1949), and subsequent White Paper (Cmnd. 8783, H.M.S.O., 1953).

Nairne, P. D., "Management and the Administrative Class" in *Public Administration*, 42 (1964), 113–22.

Ogilvy-Webb, M., *The Government Explains* (Allen & Unwin, 1965).

"Plowden Report"—*Report of the Committee on the Control of Public Expenditure* (Cmnd. 1432, H.M.S.O., 1961).

Political and Economic Planning, *Advisory Committees in British Government* (Allen & Unwin, 1960).

Co-ordination and Internal Organisation

Public Expenditure: A New Presentation (Cmnd. 4017, H.M.S.O., 1969).

Public Expenditure: Planning and Control (Cmnd. 2915, H.M.S.O., 1966).

Regan, D. E., "The Expert and the Administrator: Recent Changes at the Ministry of Transport" in *Public Administration*, 44 (1966), 149–67.

Ridley, F. F. (ed.), *Specialists and Generalists* (Allen & Unwin, 1968).

Robson, William A., "The Fulton Report on the Civil Service", in *Political Quarterly*, 39 (1968), 397–414.

Roll, Sir Eric (*et al.*), "The Machinery for Economic Planning" in *Public Administration*, 44 (1966), 1–72.

Rose, Richard (ed.), *Policy-Making in Britain* (Macmillan, 1969).

Select Committee on Estimates, Session 1957–58, Sixth Report: *Treasury Control of Expenditure* (H.C. 254, H.M.S.O., 1958).

Select Committee on Estimates, Session 1963–64, Fifth Report: *Treasury Control of Establishments* (H.C. 228, H.M.S.O., 1964).

Select Committee on Estimates, Session 1964–65, Sixth Report: *Recruitment to the Civil Service* (H.C. 308, H.M.S.O., 1965).

Self, Peter, "Reform of the Civil Service" in *Political Quarterly*, 38 (1967), 132–9, 266–75.

Shore, Peter, *Entitled to Know* (Macgibbon & Kee, 1966).

Sisson, C. H., *The Spirit of British Administration* (Faber, 2nd edn., 1966).

5. Decentralisation of Central Government

Regional Organisation of Government Departments

In its discussion of the best method of distributing governmental functions the Haldane Committee (as we have seen in Chapter 3) spent no time on organisation by place, despite the fact that a Secretary for Scotland had been exercising executive responsibilities in respect of certain aspects of Scottish affairs since 1885, while a separate Irish administration (under a Viceroy and Chief Secretary, both in the British Cabinet) was still in existence. The reason is clear. The distribution of central government functions on an area basis would throw up almost insuperable problems of co-ordination. In a sense, of course, the whole field of local government is a functional allocation by area, but this is within the context of a division—however illogical or rough and ready it may be—between central government functions on the one hand and local government functions on the other. The only *administrative* justification for the distribution of central government functions by place is that the administrative needs of an area are so distinct as to make it inconvenient or inefficient to subsume them under a centralised organisation. In a relatively small and compact territory like Britain this is an argument difficult to advance with any conviction. But this does not mean that central departments need not take account, in their organisation, of specific area needs—for example, by posting officials in the areas in order to give them direct knowledge of local problems—since the overall supervision by a single department itself provides the framework for co-ordinated policy. A further stage comes when the various departmental policies in an area are themselves co-ordinated on an area, rather than a single departmental basis.

The terminology for such a process is not altogether clear. There is, for one thing, a distinction to be made between the mere geographical dispersal of headquarters units—often undertaken because the work of the unit does not need to be performed in the London area and the government is anxious to set an example to industry of moving offices away from the overcrowded metropolis (e.g., Social Security central records office in Newcastle, the Post Office Savings Bank headquarters in Glasgow)—and the establishment of local and regional offices, which involves at least some element of delegation of discretion to the locally-based officials. Some authorities (including Mackenzie and Grove) have used the term "deconcentration" to describe headquarters dispersal and "decentralisation" to cover local and regional offices. But Wiseman, among others, feels that mere geographical dispersal of "out-stations" hardly merits a term to itself and applies "deconcentration" to delegation of authority to local and regional offices; "decentralisation" is then applied only to delegation to officials controlled, not by central departments, but by some form of elected body, as in Northern Ireland— a process which, in the older terminology, was referred to as *devolution*, involving some political as well as administrative decentralisation. Brian Smith attempts a reconciliation between the two terminologies by referring to both processes as decentralisation, one by devolution, the other by deconcentration. Thus the establishment of local and regional offices by central departments becomes "deconcentrated decentralisation", or more briefly, "field administration". The older practice is preferred here and thus by decentralisation of government departments, or administrative decentralisation, is meant, not "regional government" with elected council and regional officials, but the delegation by central departments of discretionary powers to locally-based departmental officials, particularly in the form of regional offices. This seems to be clearly a decentralising process especially if, in addition to discretionary power, regional representatives of departments participate in some form of regional

inter-departmental co-ordinating machinery for the implementation of departmental policies within the region.

In Scotland and Wales administrative decentralisation
has gone much further than in any of the English regions
since both are now served by central departments (mainly
based in Edinburgh or Cardiff but with ministerial "out-
stations" in London) with executive responsibility for some
aspects of their affairs. Thus, under the Secretary of State
for Scotland there are four Scottish departments—Home and
Health, Development, Education, and Agriculture and
Fisheries—and under the Secretary of State for Wales (an
office established in 1964) there is a small department which
is, in effect, a Welsh ministry of housing, local government,
health, and roads. It cannot be said that, in terms of strict
administrative logic, there is any overwhelming case for such
separate departmental arrangements (which must be a
prolific source of inter-departmental committees between
the Scottish and Welsh departments and their Whitehall-
based counterparts). Scotland, it is true, has retained its own
legal system and local government structure but there is no
comparable institutional difference between England and
Wales. But both Scotland and Wales have a fierce sense of
national and cultural uniqueness and it is this, rather than
administrative logic, which has determined the extent of
decentralisation. Beyond their own departmental responsibilities both Secretaries of State exercise a watching brief
over the implementation of other departmental policies in
Scotland or Wales (no doubt also largely exercised through
the medium of inter-departmental committees). In cases
where such departments have a regional organisation Scotland and Wales will have a place within it (although care is
taken to avoid the use of the word "region", and thus what
is in effect the departmental regional office will be called
"Office for Scotland" or "Office for Wales"). Wales has a
further type of decentralisation in that some London-based
departments have for long had Welsh divisions within
their headquarters organisation, either based in London or
partly or wholly based in Wales. Thus since 1907 there has
been a Welsh Department of Education within the central

ministry, and it is only comparatively recently that significant elements of the staff of the division have been based in Cardiff; from 1919 to 1968 the Welsh Board of Health in Cardiff exercised many of the functions of the Ministry of Health in Wales; and since 1920 there has been within the Ministry of Agriculture a Welsh Department of Agriculture which has always been based in Wales. It was the Welsh Office of the Ministry of Housing and Local Government which provided the main core of the newly-created Welsh Office under a Secretary of State in 1964. Curiously enough, the functions of the departments with the longest experience of administrative differentiation for Wales—Education, Agriculture, and Health—were not initially transferred to the new Secretary of State. Health and some aspects of agriculture were transferred in 1968, and the rest may follow (the Scottish equivalents are all within the executive responsibility of the Secretary of State for Scotland). It is at least conceivable, however, that a Welsh division within a central department may have more influence in shaping the detail of departmental policy than the exercise of "oversight" responsibilities by a separate Welsh department with relatively limited executive responsibilities and status (it is significant that, alone among ministerial departments in Whitehall, the permanent head of the Welsh Office is only of deputy secretary rank).

The first major development in the more limited kind of administrative decentralisation by central departments with responsibilities covering the whole of Great Britain— that of the establishment of local and regional offices—came with the setting up of labour exchanges under the Board of Trade in 1909. The local exchanges were grouped into areas, which in turn were grouped into six divisions, each under a senior official responsible for supervising the work of the local exchanges. When, in 1916, the Ministry of Labour took over this responsibility from the Board of Trade it retained and strengthened the regional system. Several of the war-time ministries, notably the Ministry of Munitions (1915), also had a regional organisation but these, unlike the Ministry of Labour, disappeared after 1918. The new Ministry of Health in 1919 set up fifteen housing regions under commissioners but these were abandoned as part of the 1922 economy measures (the "Geddes axe"). The regional offices established by the Ministry of Pensions in 1920 were, in effect, microcosms of the headquarters ministry, each having a full range of staff and responsibility for all the executive work (the ministry retaining policy control). The system lasted for six years and although considerably reduced in 1926 was not completely abolished. The Post Office in the years immediately before the outbreak of the Second World War undertook a comprehensive reorganisation of its regional organisation to effect a co-ordination of postal, telecommunications, and engineering services in each region.

The greatest impetus to administrative regionalism came with the war itself, not only in the creation of regional organisations by departments which did not already have them, but also in the perhaps more significant form of inter-departmental co-ordination within the regions. Regional Civil Defence Commissioners were set up in 1939 (based in part on the emergency transport and feeding organisation which operated during the 1926 General Strike) and although they never came to exercise the great powers in the regions which would have been theirs had Britain been invaded, they provided an administrative focal point in each region. Despite some initial reluctance (especially on the part of the Ministry of Aircraft Production and the Ministry of Supply) all the major departments eventually established regional organisations, for the most part conforming to standard regional areas based on a regional "capital" town, and stationed in them a larger number of more senior officials. The Regional Commissioners themselves provided some inter-departmental co-ordination, and there were in each region a whole range of inter-departmental committees.

The Regional Commissioners disappeared after 1945 but departmental regional organisations remained, operating in nine English regions, together with Scotland and Wales. When J. W. Grove examined the regional structure in 1950 he found that all the major departments except the Treasury still possessed some form of local or regional organisation, most working to the standard regions (which were officially demarcated by the Treasury in 1946). They included departments, like the Ministry of National Insurance (as it then was) and the Post Office, dealing directly with individual citizens; economic departments (e.g., Board of Trade, Ministry of Power) which were able to liaise with local industry through their regional offices; and departments whose responsibilities brought them into close contact with local authorities (e.g., Housing and Local Government, Education, Health, Transport, and the Home Office). The tasks given to regional offices varied from department to department but covered such activities as advice, supervision, interpretation of headquarters policy and its application to the region, inspection, and liaison with local bodies. The amount of discretion delegated to regional officers also varied considerably between departments. Departments whose work was largely of a routine character which could most easily be reduced to written codes of procedure—like those concerned with social security and revenue collection—were prepared to decentralise widely, while other departments where policy predominated over routine and where there was often difficulty in defining the extent of delegation were often reluctant to do so. The fact that one departmental regional office had to refer to headquarters matters which, in other departments, could be settled locally made more difficult the regional co-ordination of departmental policies and thus one of the advantages of decentralisation tended to be lost.

Apart from the social security and revenue departments, whose work necessarily involved contact with individuals, the tide was in fact turning against administrative regionalism at this time. The Conservative Government returned to office in 1951 was pledged to reductions in the size of the Civil Service and the running down of the staffs of local and regional offices, largely concerned with routine and executive work, had less painful consequences for policy than significant reductions in headquarters staffs. Moreover the larger local authorities and business firms (unlike smaller authorities and firms, which often found the system useful) tended to by-pass regional offices in favour of direct negotiations, either individually or through the agency of their

London-based national associations, with higher grade officials in Whitehall. Between 1949 and 1956 regional office staffs as a whole were almost halved (from over 30,000 to under 16,000), while the department most directly concerned with local authorities—the Ministry of Housing and Local Government—reduced its regional staff from 750 in 1954 to 136 in 1956, with the effect of recentralising in Whitehall almost all the department's day-to-day executive functions. Regional organisations generally had reached probably "the lowest point consistent with the convenient provision of the existing services", representing merely a difference "in scope rather than in kind" from the regional organisations which had been in existence in 1938 (Mackenzie and Grove).

The early 1960s witnessed a resurgence, however, prompted by continued evidence of unequal economic performance by particular areas of the country (as revealed, for example, in unemployment rates) and by the socio-economic problems presented by the expansion of towns and communications. In 1963 a Conservative Government White Paper, *Programme for Regional Development and Growth in the North East*, argued that central administration "will be effective only in so far as policies and decisions are informed and reinforced by regionally-based machinery", while the Buchanan Report on *Traffic in Towns*, also published in 1963, held that "the present arrangements . . . do not lend themselves to the taking of prompt initiatives on a very large scale and embracing the fields, now administratively separate, of town planning, transport, housing, and industry". In the following year Sir Keith Joseph, the Conservative Minister of Housing and Local Government, spoke of the necessity of plans for regional development involving "strong regional arms of central government".

The Conservatives left office the same year and before much could be accomplished in the provision of "strong regional arms of central government". Their Labour successors set about establishing such a machinery under the auspices, in England, of the new Department of Economic Affairs, and in Scotland and Wales of their respective Secretaries of State. Between 1964 and 1966 eight economic planning regions were set up in England—the Northern, Yorkshire and Humberside, East Midlands, East Anglia, South East, South West, West Midlands, and North West regions—one fewer than the former nine standard regions (there is no separate Southern planning region). Each region has two governmental bodies—an advisory economic planning *council* with a part-time membership of about thirty appointed from people with wide experience in the region, and a Civil Service economic planning *board*, made up of senior officials from the main government departments concerned with aspects of regional planning, under the chairmanship of an official of the Department of Economic Affairs (the equivalent bodies in Scotland and Wales are chaired by officials of the Scottish and Welsh Offices respectively although the D.E.A. is represented on them). The councils assist in the preparation, and advise on the implementation, of regional plans, and also advise on the regional implications of national economic policies and on the application in the regions of national policy. They have taken over the work of the regional boards for industry which had previously operated in each of the standard regions as local forums for discussion and advice on production matters and industrial conditions in the region. To this extent the economic planning councils are not altogether new creations, although their terms of reference are much wider and their status higher than the old regional boards (council chairmen, for example, have regular access to ministers). But the fact that they are appointed bodies with advisory functions only, and that—particularly in a small country like Britain—regional plans necessarily have implications for other regions and thus must inevitably be subject to central review, limits their effectiveness.

From the point of view of administrative decentralisation as opposed to regional government (which *elected* planning councils would imply), the regional planning boards represent a more significant institutional development. The boards have two main functions: to assist the planning council (although, of course, the board is in no sense subordinate to it), and to provide regional co-ordinating machinery for the implementation of departmental policies—they are, in effect, inter-departmental committees at the regional level (the Scottish and Welsh boards are, however, in more direct contact with the actual implementation of policies than the English boards since their chairmen report to a minister—the Secretary of State for Scotland or for Wales—who has executive responsibilities for aspects of regional planning, including town and country planning and roads: the English board chairmen report to the Secretary of State for Economic Affairs, who has no executive responsibilities). Their establishment has undoubtedly led to a strengthening of the regional organisation of departments. Most of the chairmen of the English planning boards and the chairmen of both the Scottish and Welsh boards are of under-secretary rank, and many of the other board members—the chief officers of their departments in the region—are assistant secretaries or their executive class equivalent. Administrative decentralisation, after the "recession" of the 1950s, has resumed its advance.

It remains to be seen, however, how far the regional economic planning boards have achieved a significant degree of administrative regionalism in the sense of ensuring that decisions by individual departments on developments within a particular region are co-ordinated with those of other departments and that as much decision-making as possible is carried out in the region without a continual need to refer back to headquarters in London. The boards would certainly seem to give promise of strengthening the machinery of government "by giving a greater regional content to the consideration of policy issues and providing a better instrument for working out the practical implications as it develops" (in the words of A. W. Peterson, who was the senior official in charge of regional policy at the D.E.A.). But it would be reasonable to suppose that it will take some time for the traditional vertical lines of communication between regional office and Whitehall to be replaced by the horizontal pattern provided (at any rate, potentially) by the regional boards; among other things, the fact that the individual civil servants' promotion prospects depend upon his standing with his seniors in Whitehall rather than with his colleagues from other departments in a region may well make officials reluctant to take postings to regions. The major problem will always remain of how far to decentralise without losing central control, and to this "administrative logic" can provide no clear answer. Any further development of decentralisation seems likely to come as a result of political rather than administrative pressures. The 1969 Redcliffe-Maud Report on local government in England proposed that the eight nominated English economic planning councils should be replaced by the same number of indirectly elected provincial councils, with considerably wider planning functions (in roughly the same geographical areas) and their own staffs. It anticipated that government departments would build up their regional (or, in the report's terminology, provincial) offices to match the strengthening of local government at this level. Further steps may be taken when the Commission on the Constitution, set up in 1969, has reported: this commission, unlike the Redcliffe-Maud Commission, is concerned with the whole of the United Kingdom and is not limited in its recommendations to the present division of responsibilities between central and local government. (See Appendix, p. 182.)

Public Corporations

Another method of delegating central government responsibilities is by functional decentralisation to semi-autonomous bodies. This is a process which has become an increasingly important feature of the central administrative system as government has extended its direct intervention in economic activity and as social provision has expanded. It has been felt that for these kinds of activity the full panoply of ministerial responsibility and its concomitant of parliamentary accountability is not always appropriate. Thus there has grown up a bewildering variety of *ad hoc* central administrative bodies outside the ordinary departmental structure, with widely differing degrees of autonomy, although all are ultimately the responsibility of some minister or ministers. Classifications of this heterogeneous mass have been attempted but none have succeeded in cutting a clear way through the jungle. There are bodies to regulate (like the Air Transport

Licensing Board, the Monopolies Commission and the agricultural marketing boards), bodies to sponsor or stimulate (like the Industrial Reorganisation Corporation—formed in 1966 with government finance to encourage industrial mergers—the Commonwealth Development Corporation and the British Tourist Authority), and bodies to manage (like the boards of nationalised industries and the regional hospital boards). All are performing functions which, for one reason or another, are not considered suitable for direct administration by a government department, either because of a desire to introduce a representative "user" element in the management (e.g., the Port of London Authority), to associate local authorities and other local bodies with a service which must still be administered centrally (e.g., the regional hospital boards), to facilitate the participation of private commercial or industrial interests (e.g., agricultural marketing boards, the British Standards Institution, the Council for Industrial Design), or to allow of the maximum commercial and managerial freedom in the running of an industry or public service which has been brought into complete public ownership.

Somewhere embedded in this multiplicity of organisations is the concept of a *public corporation*, which W. A. Robson has hailed as "the most important constitutional innovation which has been evolved in Great Britain" in the twentieth century. The trouble is that the concept is by no means clear. A government department is a relatively easy administrative unit to differentiate. It is wholly staffed by civil servants and dependent on a parliamentary vote for its expenditure. A public corporation is more difficult to delineate. It may be headed by a board or group of commissioners, controlling a staff which is not included within the Civil Service. A minister, or ministers, normally appoints the members of the board and has general policy control over its operations, leaving day-to-day matters of administration in the hands of the board or commission. The degree of ministerial control varies widely, however, and where it is greatest the corporation most resembles a government department. Thus the Forestry Commission, although formally headed by a paid part-time chairman and unpaid part-time commissioners, is in reality little more than a specialised section of the Ministry of Agriculture—and indeed its permanent staff was included among the Civil Service for the purpose of Treasury statistics until 1965. Similarly the British Council, almost wholly dependent on government grants, is more a minor department than an independent body, and the same may be said of the Land Commission set up in 1967. On the other hand, the day-to-day operations of one of the longest-established corporations, the British Broadcasting Corporation, are almost completely free from ministerial interference, despite the fact that its finances depend largely upon the proportion of the broadcasting licence revenue allowed to it by the Postmaster General.

The related question of what bodies should be included in the category of public corporations is also a difficult one (and the treatment that follows is in no sense intended to be comprehensive). Some authorities seem to count as a public corporation any body with a corporate personality established by statute. This leads to the absurdity of including the Hairdressers Council set up under the Hairdressers Registration Act of 1964 in a list of recently-established public corporations. On a less trivial level the same list (by J. F. Garner) includes the National Board for Prices and Incomes, first set up in 1965 and put on a statutory basis in 1966. But whether statutory or not this body seems much more an arbitral arm of the government's prices and incomes policy, or a particular type of government advisory body, than what would ordinarily be understood by a "public corporation". While it is impossible to be precise a public corporation would seem essentially to involve some kind of management or regulation, either of a commercial or industrial concern or of a public utility or social service. Griffith and Street make a rough distinction between corporations which are "managerial-economic"—including the great industrial and commercial corporations set up after 1945—and those which are "managerial-social", including the regional hospital boards which control most of the hospital provision within the national health service, and the new town development corporations (together with the New Towns Commission set up in 1959). The discussion here is concerned primarily with the "managerial-economic" corporations which—in form at least—have a more autonomous position than regional hospital boards and the development corporations. The latter are rather *ad hoc* local administrative units of national policy directly supervised by Whitehall departments (on somewhat similar lines to nineteenth-century poor law boards and school boards, except that they are not elected) than public corporations, although they are usually ranked as such.

The first clear-cut examples of public corporations in the commercial or industrial fields came after the First World War (the Port of London Authority, established in 1908 as the only alternative to granting the necessary monopoly power for dock development to one of the private companies owning the docks, was limited in area and function, as was the even older Mersey Docks and Harbour Board—although they both rank as public corporations). The Central Electricity Board was established in 1926 to concentrate and rationalise electricity generation without taking over the power stations, to build and operate a main transmission system or national grid, to buy the output of selected power stations and to sell it to the many local undertakings for distribution. In the following year the British Broadcasting Corporation was established by royal charter to provide a national broadcasting service free from either commercial or direct governmental influence, and in 1933 the London Passenger Transport Board was created to operate as a single undertaking the whole complex public passenger transport system of the London metropolitan area, excluding the main surface railways. The development of air transport was from the first dependent upon government subsidies and the private operators were thus subject to considerable government influence and control. In 1939 a single public corporation, British Overseas Airways Corporation, was formed to take over the two main subsidised air transport companies.

But the real impetus came in 1945 when the new Labour Government decided to use the public corporation as the main instrument for its programme of nationalising the main basic industries. Alternative methods of bringing the industries into public ownership—administration by a government department (as with postal and telecommunications service, ordnance factories, and naval dockyards), local authority (as with pre-nationalisation local gas and electricity undertakings), or "mixed enterprise" in which the government held a substantial part of the share capital (as with the British Petroleum Company and the British Sugar Corporation, for example)—were all rejected. The "Post Office model" was rejected largely because of the general distrust of the ability of a government department, operating within the framework of full parliamentary accountability and Treasury control, to manage efficiently a large-scale commercial or industrial enterprise. (A subsidiary reason related to the subject matter of the first part of this chapter—the difficulty a government department has in decentralising. It was felt that a large-scale industrial concern, unlike a department, could be split up into largely independent units if necessary.) Nationalisation by local authority was never really considered seriously since local areas were thought to be too small, and indeed the nationalisation process as carried out involved the transfer of municipal gas and electricity undertakings to large-scale area boards. A "mixed enterprise" organisation seemed inappropriate for the nationalisation of such basic industries as coal, gas, electricity, and transport, which had in any case long been subject to a considerable degree of governmental control (particularly the coal industry and the railways) on lines somewhat akin to that of a "mixed enterprise" and which had already proved inadequate.

Although "nationalisation" was a matter of acute party controversy at the time there was a widespread recognition that there were respectable non-doctrinal reasons for nationalising the Bank of England (this was virtually unopposed), coal, gas, electricity, and inland and civil air transport (there was much less agreement on the necessity to nationalise the iron and steel industry—the last of the 1945–51 Labour Government's nationalisation measures): the undesirability of leaving a basic industrial *monopoly*, however well-regulated, in private hands; and the limitations of private enterprise in undertaking the necessary—and costly—research and development. Once the idea of nationalisation was, perforce, accepted the political parties in the 1945–50 Parliament were united in their preference for the public corporation (a device which Conservative or Conservative-dominated governments had utilised before the war) over the government department. For those on the political "right" the public corporation was seen as the application of the company form of management, with the emphasis on the managers being free from political interference, while those on the "left" saw the corporation as a public body operating in the public interest and not merely for private profit. Thus when a Conservative Government succeeded the Labour Government in 1951 it contented itself with "denationalising" only iron and steel (brought into public ownership once more in 1967) and road haulage, while itself later establishing new corporations to—among other things—supervise research and development in nuclear energy (the United Kingdom Atomic Energy Authority) and regulate independent commercial television companies (the Independent Television Authority).

One of the most important administrative aspects of the post-1945 public corporations is the degree of ministerial control. The two most closely analogous pre-war corporations—the Central Electricity Board and the London Passenger Transport Board—placed the emphasis on the independence of the directing board from political or Civil Service supervision. The business was to be run as nearly as possible on the lines of the best private concerns. Thus capital was raised on the open market without Treasury guarantee; members of the Central Electricity Board, although appointed by the Minister (at first, of Transport and later, of Fuel and Power), were given statutory security of tenure of not less than five years; while members of the London Passenger Transport Board, who also enjoyed statutory security of tenure, were appointed, not by the minister but by the curious device (not subsequently repeated) of "Appointing Trustees"—who included the chairman of the London County Council, the chairman of the committee of London clearing banks, the president of the Law Society, and the president of the Institute of Chartered Accountants—to ensure political impartiality. Even in the case of the heavily-subsidised B.O.A.C. the responsible minister (the Secretary of State for Air) had no general power of direction, although there were specific powers exercisable during the period of the subsidy.

The post-1945 corporations provide ministers with considerably more opportunities for control. Theoretically managerial freedom and initiative is guaranteed by making the corporations independent in their "day-to-day administration" and subject to the minister only in matters of "general policy". But in practice the dichotomy between policy and administration has been as difficult to observe in the relations between ministers and corporations as in other areas of public administration (e.g., the respective roles of ministers and civil servants in the "policy-making" process). As has been often pointed out, "The process of policy-formation takes place at a number of different levels and no one can say where the 'general' ends and the 'day-to-day' begins" (A. H. Hanson).

Although there are many individual variations in the nationalisation measures the general pattern of statutory powers for the responsible minister is more or less standard: and the powers are extensive. The minister usually appoints the chairman and members of the board, makes regulations on their tenure of office, and has power to re-appoint them at the end of their term of office. He can dismiss a board member if "in the opinion of the Minister he becomes unfit to continue in office or incapable of performing his duties" (the minister's powers over the tenure of board members are in fact considerably stronger than that over their senior departmental officials). Then the minister has the formal power to issue general policy directives: "The Minister may, after consultations with the Board, give to the Board directions of a general character as to the exercise and performance by the Board of their functions in relation to matters appearing to the Minister to affect the national interest, and the Board shall give effect to any such directions." There are obvious interpretative difficulties about this formulation—for example, the

precise meanings of "general character" and "national interest"—but there is no mistaking the formal position of
superiority in which it places the minister. It is worth noting,
moreover, that the statutory mention of a power to issue mandatory directive does not preclude the use of informal methods
of influence: a distinguished judge—Lord Denning—believes
that the power to give directives was inserted as a safety pre-
caution *in case* the corporation should not prove amenable to
ministers' policy suggestions (*Tamlin v. Hannaford*, 1950).
The minister may, in addition, require the board to furnish
him with any information he needs regarding the property and
activities of the board, he determines the form of their annual
accounts, appoints auditors, and lays their annual report
(which is submitted to him) before Parliament. He enters
importantly into capital development and borrowing: where
a substantial outlay on capital account is involved, the board
must act on lines settled with the minister's approval; moreover, since 1956 no stock has been issued and the corporations rely for their borrowing on interest-bearing Exchequer
loans negotiated through the minister with the approval of
the Treasury. These are more or less general powers. There
are also powers specific to particular nationalised industries,
such as the Minister of Power's power to define and vary the
areas of the gas and electricity area boards (the same minister
has a total of fifty-six specific responsibilities under the legislation nationalising the fuel and power industries).

All these are formal powers, for which ministers are
accountable to Parliament (the question of the parliamentary
accountability of the nationalised industries is discussed in
Chapter 7). But in the actual operation of the corporations as
opposed to their formal legislative framework (as in the working of political constitutions) a whole series of "conventions"
has grown up in the relations between ministers and boards,
the total effect of which is to increase the power of ministers,
without, however, increasing their accountability to Parliament. W. A. Robson believes that the legal powers are a less
important means of influence than that "exercised informally
through discussion, negotiation and pressure" while A. H.
Hanson has observed that "it can hardly be said that the

corporations enjoy that freedom from ministerial interference which was originally envisaged for them".

The first overt evidence of informal ministerial intervention in what seemed a matter of day-to-day administration was the revelation in the first annual report of the nationalised electricity industry (for 1947–9) that the Minister of Fuel and Power (Hugh Gaitskell) had compelled the board, against its better judgement, to adopt a winter surcharge on electricity—the so-called "Clow differential"—in an effort to cut consumption (it was later abandoned). There was no formal directive, merely an expression of the minister's wishes: but as Hanson has said, "the distinction between consulting with a minister and receiving a ministerial order is so fine as to be almost imperceptible". Since then the numerous reports of the Select Committee on the Nationalised Industries (see Chapter 7) from 1957 have documented the process in great detail while a report issued in 1968 was entirely devoted to the general question of ministerial control. Its 1958 report on the coal industry, for example, spoke of regular meetings between the Ministry of Power and the National Coal Board to keep the industry's investment programme and progress under continuous review, weekly discussions of production figures and daily discussions of "all problems"; and recorded that the board had informally agreed not to raise the general level of prices—statutorily a board matter—without the minister's agreement (the 1961 committee report on the gas industry recorded a similar extra-statutory ministerial control over gas prices). In the following year (1959) the report on the air corporations (B.O.A.C. and B.E.A.) catalogued a "formidable collection" of unofficial ministerial powers: "Thus, although the Minister has no express statutory control over the Corporations' capital expenditure, they always seek his approval (and that of the Treasury) for orders of aircraft, and these amount to 80 per cent of their total capital expenditure. They have agreed not to open new routes without the Minister's consent. They fly on various routes, domestic and international, because he asks them to, and they lose money in the process. They seek his approval for all fares and rates on non-international routes. They refrain, at his wish, from keeping aircraft specifically available for charter work. They come to him for permission before creating or investing in a subsidiary company and, in effect, get his authority before they dispose of such an investment." The committee felt "bound to ask" if the total extent of the minister's non-statutory powers "do not add up to a degree of control far in excess of that envisaged by the statutes under which B.O.A.C. and B.E.A. were created, and so lead to an undesirable diminution in the authority of the Chairman and Boards of the Corporations and in their feeling of responsibility". When, some five years later (1964), the committee re-examined the B.O.A.C. alone, it found evidence to show that the Ministry of Aviation had successfully pressed B.O.A.C. to increase its order for new jet aircraft (VC-10s) in the interests of the air-craft manufacturing industry (the Air Corporations Act of 1966 gave statutory authority to the minister in this field). A similar story of detailed ministerial control was observed by the committee in the nationalised rail industry (in its 1960 report), although it was this industry which had received two of the very few *formal* ministerial directives—in 1952 and 1956, both occasions involving forbidding or delaying increases in rail fares and rates. The committee's 1968 report on minis-terial control of the nationalised industries concluded that ministers and departments sponsoring particular industries (e.g., the Ministry of Power and coal, gas, electricity, and steel; the Ministry of Transport and the railways; the Board of Trade and the air corporations) had in fact been doing almost precisely the opposite of what had been envisaged in the nationalisation statutes. Although they were supposed to lay down policies to guide the operations of the industries but not to intervene in the managerial implementation of those policies, they had in practice become closely involved in many aspects of management without, however, giving the industries any very clear policy guidance.

The crux of the government-nationalised industry re-lationship is in the possibility of conflict between the board's commercial judgement and the government's economic and social policy. It would be unrealistic to expect that a govern-ment wishing to exert direct influence on the economy could afford to neglect asserting control over the nationalised industries sector (accounting for about 11 per cent of the gross domestic product and employing some 8 per cent of the total national labour force) which *ipso facto* may be expected to be more responsive to such influences than is the private sector. Much of the ministerial intervention has in fact been concerned with the corporations' pricing policy since, although statutorily they determine their own prices, a government aiming at trying to maintain stable prices over the economy as a whole (as governments have increasingly done) cannot fail to have an interest in the price levels of the virtually monopoly products and services of publicly-owned industries. Social considerations also arise. The nationalised industries exist primarily to provide a public service, not to make a profit, and this will involve sometimes providing essential but uneconomic services which would not be provided by private enterprise (e.g., electrification in rural areas, maintaining under-used rail routes where there is no alternative method of public transport).

But although the nationalised industries have no statutory obligation to make a profit, the original legislation which established them did envisage their "breaking even" over a period, taking one year with another. A White Paper on the *Financial and Economic Obligations of the Nationalised Industries,* published in April 1961, defined the general financial objectives in more detail. The government's general policy, the White Paper pointed out, is to ensure that the industries are organised and administered efficiently and economically. They are not to be regarded as social services absolved from economic and commercial obligations: they are expected to pay their way, with surpluses in some years available to meet deficits in other years. They cannot, however, "be regarded only as large commercial concerns which may be judged mainly on their commercial results: all have, although in varying degrees, wider obligations than commercial concerns in the private sector". The White Paper lays three general requirements on the corporations: (1) to pay their way over a period of five years; (2) to earn enough to yield at least 6 per cent on the money invested in them, that is, to cover the cost of borrowing money for them; and (3) to set aside money for use as a safeguard against unforeseen contingencies and for capital development. Subsequently, specific individual financial objectives were set for each industry, usually expressed as a percentage return on net assets. The two exceptions were both industries which had unique financial difficulties: the National Coal Board merely had the obligation to break even, while the British Railways Board had the statutory duty (under legislation of 1962) to reduce the railways' deficit and break even "as soon as possible". (The Select Committee on Nationalised Industries pointed out in its 1963 report that there was no specific *statutory* authority to set financial targets; as regards the air corporations this authority was given in the Air Corporations Act, 1966.)

A further White Paper in November 1967 considerably refined the criteria for the investment and pricing policies of the industries. New investment projects will have to show either that they will justify their initial cost (discounting future returns at a rate of 8 per cent, later raised to 10 per cent) or that there is some special social or wider justification: thus, for example, extensions to the London underground railway network may reduce congestion costs, while social and regional benefits may be derived from keeping open non-economic railway branch lines. Nationalised industry price increases may now be referred to the National Board for Prices and Incomes (in the same way as those in private industry) but the role of that board will be to check on the efficiency of management in cutting costs, the timing of increases, and the general justification for higher prices, within the framework of the financial objectives laid down for the particular nationalised industry. The pricing system will now be geared to the cost of supplying extra units of the product or service—the marginal cost—rather than, as previously, to the simple average cost of all units in use; the assumption being that marginal cost pricing is the only method which in principle yields the optimum use of resources since demand is then set at the level at which the cost of extra supply begins to exceed the price people will pay.

The other important departure in the 1967 White Paper

is directly relevant to the question of the extent of ministerial control: it establishes clear principles for recognising the wider economic and social obligations of the nationalised industries. It is acknowledged in the White Paper that the corporations have a right—and duty—to take these considerations into account, but only in so far as they do so in a way which does not undermine normal financial discipline in management. Thus any departure from commercial principles will be made only on specific government responsibility. The aim will be to do it openly, and a specific subsidy or adjustment of financial target will be made to take account of the particular decision. The fact that ministers in the past have intervened, often indirectly and in private, to persuade corporations to take decisions on non-commercial criteria has been a fertile source of complaint, and if the guide-lines laid down in the White Paper are fully implemented it may be that this particular difficulty will be alleviated. Indeed, the White Paper specifically re-affirmed the government's intention not to interfere in the day-to-day management of the industries.

The report on ministerial control issued by the Select Committee on Nationalised Industries warmly welcomed the 1967 White Paper as providing the basis for constructing a new economic framework which would give the industries the guidance they require in carrying out both their commercial and public interest obligations. But it needed to be supplemented by institutional changes to provide a clear separation between the two purposes of ministerial control: that of securing the wider public interest and that of overseeing the efficiency of the industries. This would best be achieved, in the committee's view, by replacing the sponsoring ministers by a single Minister of the Nationalised Industries, who would be responsible for supervising and seeking to ensure commercial and managerial efficiency, leaving other ministers with the responsibility for the formulation and application of wider policies relating to or affecting the industries (e.g., the Minister of Transport and general transport policy). Thus the Minister of the Nationalised Industries would, among other things, appoint and dismiss board members, lay down pricing and investment policies, agree financial objectives, approve investment projects, capital structure and borrowings, initiate efficiency studies, and account to Parliament for the activities of the industries as commercial bodies. Other departments would remain responsible for initiating policies to secure wider public interests—wider, that is, than the purely commercial interests of the industries as judged by the industries themselves. The Department of Employment and Productivity or the Department of Economic Affairs might, for example, promote the use of coal in electricity power stations in order to prevent unemployment in mining areas or too rapid a run-down in the coal industry. But the committee thought it important that in all such cases the department concerned should be responsible for any payments or compensation to the industry providing the service.

The committee's recommendation clearly raises formidable organisational problems, of the type already discussed in Chapter 3. In evidence to the committee the Treasury maintained that it was not possible to separate responsibility for securing the public interest from that of seeing that the industries are efficiently run—and the point seems a valid one. It also remains open to doubt whether a single Ministry of the Nationalised Industries would in fact lead to less onerous ministerial intervention in day-to-day management than the existing system. It thus came as no surprise when the government later announced its rejection of this particular recommendation.

Public corporations running vast industrial or commercial enterprises throw up unique problems of internal organisation which can be referred to only briefly here. There is, for example, the question of the degree of authority exercised by the central board over area administrative units. The original statutory framework ranged from the highly centralised National Coal Board, which was left free to determine its own divisional organisation, to the decentralised gas industry, the assets of which were vested in the twelve area gas boards which alone had the power to produce and supply gas, leaving the central Gas Council with general supervisory and borrowing powers (it was given somewhat greater powers by legislation passed in 1965). Many organisational changes have been made subsequently in all the industries, often as a result of the report of *ad hoc* committees of investigation, like the Fleck Report on the coal industry (1955) and the Herbert Report on the electricity supply industry (1956). The latest nationalisation measure—that for the renationalised iron and steel industry in 1967—has (like its short-lived predecessor of 1949) emphasised the operational autonomy of the companies taken over.

Another frequently discussed organisational problem is whether the board should be solely concerned with top-level policy decisions in the industry or whether its members should, in addition, have specific managerial functions (which also involves their being full-time). No generally-accepted solution has been found. Practice varies from corporation to corporation, and even within the same corporation at different times. The National Coal Board, for example, was functional when established in 1946 but subsequently most members shed their specific executive responsibilities; after the Fleck Report in 1955, however, the functional principle was reintroduced. A related problem concerns recruitment to the boards. Many senior appointments have of necessity to be made from outside the corporations and if the level of management ability is to be maintained—or improved—it would seem essential for the salary levels to be sufficiently high to attract industrialists from the private sector. Until recent years the salaries of chairmen, deputy chairmen, and most full-time board members were usually somewhat above those of the most senior civil servants but noticeably below those of their counterparts in private industry (they were raised in 1969 for the first time since 1964). The result has been that when the government wished to attract a particular industrial figure to the chairmanship of a public corporation it sometimes had to pay a salary considerably in excess of the norm for other corporation appointments, as when Lord Beeching became chairman of the British Transport Commission (and later of the British Railways Board) in 1961. Most members of the Steel Corporation formed in 1967 received far higher salaries than the most highly-paid chairmen of already established corporations, while in 1968 a deputy chairman was appointed to the British Railways Board at a higher salary than the chairman. A high general level of remuneration for board members would seem to be essential if the flow between the private and the public sectors is to continue and—at least as important—if there is to be a proper series of differentials between the various levels of management to spur ambition throughout the enterprise.

Public ownership through the medium of a public corporation was thought by many to involve more than opportunities for ministerial control or parliamentary accountability. Some of the industries which were nationalised—notably coal—had poor labour relations records, and it was hoped that the new framework would induce a more favourable atmosphere for industrial relations. There is no clear evidence that it has done so, and indeed the nationalised industries have had their full share of labour disputes. The role of the consumer has also not developed in the way that had been hoped, despite the elaborate organisation of consumer councils which exists in every industry. It is through the traditional political controls of minister and Parliament, rather than that of workers or consumers, that the concept of public ownership has been expressed in the nationalised industries.

It is still too early to be sure that the public corporation has established itself as the organ of management for nationalised industries and public services. Two leading academic authorities, W. A. Robson and A. H. Hanson, differ in their attitudes to the implications of the growth of informal ministerial control. Robson (a firm supporter of the public corporation idea) believes that the formal powers given to ministers are quite sufficient to enable them to exercise their proper responsibilities and that they should not be permitted "to remain in the twilight zone" of informal discussion and pressure without the necessity of disclosing to the public or to Parliament the real extent of their intervention. Hanson, on the other hand, considers that the government cannot divest itself of responsibility for any aspect of the performance of a nationalised industry, whether it be subsumed under "general policy", "commercial judgement" or "day-to-day administration". The arguments in favour of nationalisation by government department rather than by public corporation are, he feels, "very much stronger than the original advocates were prepared to allow". But Hanson sees virtue in relieving the industries of full ministerial responsibility, with its concomitant of Treasury control, and favours an intermediate position between a (theoretically) autonomous public corporation and a traditional government department. This is a view which has received a good deal of support and thus the decision, announced in 1966, to convert the Post Office (which had in 1961 been relieved of the full rigours of Treasury control) into a public corporation seemed somewhat against the trend. But the new Post Office organisation, which came into operation in October 1969, could well turn out to be the kind of "half-way house" which Hanson envisaged. (See Appendix, p. 182.)

For Further Reading

1. *Regional Organisation of Government Departments*

British Imperial Calendar and Civil Service List (H.M.S.O., annually).

Department of Economic Affairs, *Economic Planning in the Regions* (C.O.I., 2nd edn., 1968).

Grove, J. W., *English Regional Government: A Study of the North-West* (Royal Institute of Public Administration, 1951).

Grove, J. W., *Regional Administration* (Gollancz, 1951).

Joseph, Sir Keith, "Local Authorities and Regions" in *Public Administration*, 42 (1964), 215–26.

Mackenzie, W. J. M., and Grove, J. W., *Central Administration in Britain* (Longmans, 1957). Chapter 16.

Mackintosh, John P., *The Devolution of Power* (Chatto & Windus, 1968).

Mackintosh, John P., "Regional Administration: has it worked in Scotland?" in *Public Administration*, 42 (1964), 253–75.

Peterson, A. W., "Regional Economic Planning Councils and Boards" in *Public Administration*, 44 (1966), 29–41.

Select Committee on Estimates, Session 1953–54, Sixth Report: *Regional Organisations of Government Departments* (H.C. 233, H.M.S.O., 1954).

Smith, Brian C., *Field Administration* (Routledge & Kegan Paul, 1967).

Smith, Brian C., *Regionalism in England* (three pamphlets) (Acton Society Trust, 1964–5).

Wiseman, H. Victor, "Regional Government in the United Kingdom" in *Parliamentary Affairs*, XIX (1966), 56–82.

2. *Public Corporations*

Britain: An official Handbook (H.M.S.O., annually).

Chester, D. N., "The Nationalised Industries" in The *Three Banks Review* (December 1952), 23–46.

Chester, D. N., "Public Corporations and the Classification of Administrative Bodies" in *Political Studies*, 1 (1953), 34–52.

Coombes, David, *The Member of Parliament and the Administration: The Case of the Select Committee on Nationalised Industries* (Allen & Unwin, 1966).

Financial and Economic Obligations of the Nationalised Industries (Cmnd. 1337, H.M.S.O., 1961).

Garner, J. F., "New Public Corporations" in *Public Law* (1966), 324–9.

Griffith, J. A. G., and Street, H., *Principles of Administrative Law* (Pitman, 4th edn., 1967). Chapter VII.

Hanson, A. H., "Ministers and Boards" in *Public Administration*, 47 (1969), 65–74.

Hanson, A. H. (ed.), *Nationalisation: A Book of Readings* (Allen & Unwin, 1963).

Hanson, A. H., *Parliament and Public Ownership* (Cassell, 2nd edn., 1962).

Kelf-Cohen, R., *Twenty Years of Nationalisation: The British Experience* (Macmillan, 1969).

Nationalised Industries: A Review of Economic and Financial Objectives (Cmnd. 3437, H.M S.O., 1967).

Robson, William A., *Nationalised Industry and Public Ownership* (Allen & Unwin, 2nd edn., 1962).

Select Committee on Nationalised Industries (Reports and Accounts). Various reports issued from 1957, especially session 1967–68, First Report: *Ministerial Control of the Nationalised Industries* (H.C. 371, 3 vols., H.M.S.O., 1968), and the government's reply to this report (Cmnd. 4027, H.M.S.O., 1969).

Street, Sir Arthur, "Quasi-Government Bodies since 1918" in Campion, Sir Gilbert (*et al.*), *British Government since 1918* (Allen & Unwin, 1950).

Thornhill, W., *The Nationalised Industries* (Nelson, 1968).

Tivey, Leonard J., *Nationalisation in British Industry* (Cape, 1966).

6. Administration
by Local Authorities

In total local authorities—spending each year about a third of all public expenditure and employing some 8 per cent of the national labour force—represent a most important sector of public administration, while large individual authorities, like Greater London, Birmingham, and Lancashire, constitute single administrative structures more complex and wide-ranging than those of several independent States. An account of administrative procedure in local government cannot be omitted from a review of public administration, however brief. The difficulty is, however, that while generalisations can be made about local government—for example, about the vital relationship with central government—they remain generalisations and as such need qualification in their application to individual authorities. And it is, of course, impossible to examine each of the over 1,400 local authorities in England and Wales, excluding some 11,000 minor authorities (parishes and rural boroughs), to discover their individual administrative practices (it is not proposed to refer specifically here to the slightly different local government system in Scotland, with over 400 authorities, but much of the general analysis of English local government is applicable also to Scotland). For long, indeed, the study of local government was more concerned with the formal legal structure than with what actually went on in local authorities—a process which made it easier to ignore individual variations. It is only in recent years that substantial evidence has been accumulated of specific administrative practice in representative local authorities: studies, for example, of the effects of party organisation on the work of local authorities, J. A. G. Griffith's study of the substance of central-local relations and, most importantly, the material assembled by the Maud Committee on the Management of Local Government (which reported in May 1967, two months after the parallel Mallaby Committee on Staffing) and the Royal Commission on Local Government in England, under the chairmanship of Lord Redcliffe-Maud, which deliberated from 1966 to 1969. Generalisations about local authority administration can now be grounded in vastly more empirical data than was possible only a few years ago.

Local authorities represent a decentralisation both by area and by function and in this have some affinity with the local and regional organisation of government departments and with public corporations (local authorities are in fact corporations). The distinction is that local authorities, unlike regional offices or public corporations, are multi-functional and run by elected councils. The analogy is somewhat closer with Whitehall and Westminster. The local council parallels Parliament in its supervision of the work of a range of local departments and while there is no formal local parallel for the departmental minister and the Cabinet there is the local committee system which, in large urban authorities run on strict party political lines, can operate in a way not altogether dissimilar from a "Cabinet system" (one of the steps in the evolution of Ceylon towards the "Westminster model"— the so-called Donoughmore Constitution of 1931—involved a system resembling English local authority committees). The main distinction here concerns powers. Local authorities, unlike Parliament, have no legislative autonomy and indeed hardly rank as legislative bodies at all. Local authorities must be able to point to specific statutory sanction for all their activities and their freedom is thus circumscribed by the principle of *ultra vires:* the possibility of external control—by the courts, by Parliament and by government departments— lies behind all they do. And beyond that there is, of course, accountability to the local electorate, with elections taking place (at least every three years and sometimes annually) rather more frequently than parliamentary elections.

Local government in the British context has meant government of local affairs by elected local councils—local self-government—historically because the main development of modern local government (as incorporated in such statutes as the Municipal Corporation Acts of 1835 and 1882 and the Local Government Acts of 1888 and 1894) was at a time when the traditions of liberal democracy—extension of the right to vote, secrecy of the ballot, and so on—were also being laid down. Thus even when functions were given in the nineteenth century not to existing local authorities but to *ad hoc* bodies (e.g., poor law boards and school boards) these were also elected. There is, of course, nothing inevitable about elected local institutions: it would be perfectly possible for local administration to be in the hands, for example, of bodies with a membership nominated by the central government. They might not be as responsive to local pressures but there is no reason to believe that such a system would be necessarily less efficient or less humane. But it is widely felt that local self-government has a justification beyond the administrative efficiency it may—or may not—bring to the conduct of community affairs: that it diffuses political responsibility and widens participation in public life.

Similarly, there is nothing inevitable about the division of responsibilities between central government—departments and their local and regional organisation, public corporations and other semi-autonomous central bodies—and local authorities. Local functions have been more the result of chronology than logic. Institutions of local government such as the historic units of county, borough, and parish have existed for centuries and it was natural that they should be used in the administration of central legislation on such broad social matters as public assistance, public health and, eventually, education. Indeed central government was largely skeletal for much of the nineteenth century and units of local administration of centrally-supervised services had either to be the existing local authorities or bodies, like poor law and school boards, specially created for the purpose. It was not until the structure of local government had been reformed by the legislation of 1888–94 that the main *ad hoc* bodies in the local field disappeared and their functions were taken over by the new local councils.

For much of the nineteenth century local authorities carried out their main responsibilities with real if varying autonomy but the twentieth century has seen a progressive official recognition of the fact that many local authority functions, and certainly the most important of them, are national rather than local. Thus the report of the Royal Commission on Taxation in 1901 made a distinction between "national and onerous" local functions like poor relief, education, police, and main roads—which should be a charge as much upon the national taxpayer as upon the local ratepayer—and "local and beneficial" functions which should be wholly supported by local rates. Since then the process of "nationalising" local services has proceeded apace, especially with the great expansion of social services following the Second World War. The Education Act of 1944, for example, gives the minister the duty "to secure the effective execution by local authorities, under his control and direction, of the national policy for providing a varied and comprehensive educational service in every area"; the National Health Service Act of 1946 describes the personal health services of local authorities as part of the National Health Service; the Children Act of 1948 provides that "local authorities shall exercise their functions . . . under the general guidance of the Secretary of State"; the Public Libraries and Museums Act of 1964 charges the minister with the duty to "superintend and promote the improvement of the public library service provided by local authorities in England and Wales, and to secure the proper discharge by local authorities of the functions in relation to libraries conferred on them as library authorities"; and the Police Act of 1964 provides that "the Secretary of State shall exercise his powers in a way which appears to him to be best calculated to promote the efficiency of the police".

Local authorities are no longer autonomous and their activities and organisation cannot be understood except in terms of the all-pervading relationship with central government. But however dependent local authorities may be on central government for direction, control, and finance, it is they, not the central government, which actually provide the services—run schools, build roads, acquire land, build houses, administer local health services, and so on. Ministers (and their departments) influence but they do not provide the services which are statutorily vested in local authorities. In some cases local functions are expressly vested in a minister, and then he—not a local authority—becomes responsible for carrying them out, as with trunk roads and motorways (for which local authorities may act as *agents* of the Ministry of Transport), the new towns set up by the Minister of Housing and Local Government (and administered by public corporations), and the Home Secretary's supervision of the Metropolitan Police. Otherwise the local authorities are still autonomous as administrative units, exercising their responsibilities in their own right, not as agents of government departments.

Internal Organisation

Local authorities enjoy their greatest freedom from central control in matters of internal organisation, which is essentially based upon the relationship of part-time elected council members and officials, working primarily through a system of committees. The committees, mainly of councillors but also often including some co-opted members from outside the council, supervise the work of the local officials organised in departments: the basic pattern is of a committee and a corresponding department for each major service or function (or related group of functions).

Internal organisation is by no means free from statutory provision, however. The law prescribes the procedure for the conduct of a local authority's meetings and the expenses and allowances payable to members. The accounts of local authorities (except some accounts of some borough councils outside Greater London) are subject to auditors appointed by the Minister of Housing and Local Government and the accounting procedure for accounts thus subject to district audit is controlled by law. The district auditor has a duty to disallow every item in the accounts which is contrary to law (including those which he considers "unreasonable") and to surcharge the amount of any expenditure disallowed upon the council members responsible for incurring or authorising the expenditure. And there is evidence that the possibility of surcharge does unduly inhibit the actions of an authority.

There are also legal provisions regarding committees and officers but these are far from comprehensive in their operation, indeed seem almost arbitrary and erratic. Thus county and county borough councils must constitute education, health, welfare, and children's committees, while county councils must have finance committees. These are all important functions, but other important functions—like housing, town and country planning, and highways—do not involve the same statutory requirement, while committees are statutory for quite minor functions (e.g., smallholdings, allotments, diseases of animals). A local authority could hardly organise its committee structure merely on those statutorily required but the fact that some are mandatory does inevitably affect the flexibility of its internal arrangements.

Similarly the appointment of certain officers is prescribed by law. Under the Local Government Act of 1933 all authorities must appoint a clerk, a treasurer, a surveyor, and a medical officer of health and all except counties a public health inspector; and the appointment of a medical officer of health or a public health inspector cannot be terminated without ministerial consent. Specific legislation requires counties and county boroughs to appoint a chief education officer and a children's officer, in each case in consultation with the minister, who may veto an appointment. Under the Police Act of 1964 appointments of chief constables, deputy chief constables, and assistant chief constables have to be approved by the Home Secretary. Again, an authority obviously needs to appoint many more officers than those statutorily required but another element of inflexibility is introduced, although not nearly as serious as that implicit in statutory committees.

Beyond these rather sporadic statutory provisions is an even more significant requirement of the 1933 Local Government Act—that the local council cannot delegate its functions to individual members or to officers: " . . . all acts of a local authority and all questions coming before a local authority shall be done and decided by a majority of the members of the local authority present and voting thereon at a meeting of the local authority". But councils are often large (some are over 150, with the average for county councils eighty-six and county boroughs fifty-seven) and this, added to the part-time nature of council membership, compels the establishment of committees—perhaps the most characteristic feature of the administration of British local authorities. But the committees are delegatees of the council and if their recommendations are normally to be accepted by that body their composition needs to reflect the composition of the whole council, which retains the formal executive responsibility for all the authority's work. Moreover, although the law allows a local authority to delegate its functions to committees, it does not provide for their delegation to officers. There is thus a clear distinction between a senior civil servant, acting in the name of his minister, and a chief officer in local government. The chief officer cannot at his discretion exercise the powers of the council; in law and in most actual cases a resolution of the council or one of its committees is needed to support his action.

The law, for the most part, leaves to the individual local authority the determination of a whole series of internal relationships, such as those between committees and the council, between committee and committee, between elected members and officials, and between various officials. It is possible to see a basic pattern over the whole range of local authorities but there are many individual variations.

The committees submit recommendations to the council, very few of which are normally referred back or rejected, but they may in addition exercise powers delegated to them by the council (but which, of course, are always subject to review by the council if that body desires it). A committee's work may range from important matters of policy, such as the determination of the scope and organisation of a department's work, to relatively minor matters, such as (to quote from the Maud Committee report): "interviewing for appointments (even at assistant caretaker level in some cases), authorising repairs to buildings, granting leave to employees to attend courses, deciding on furnishings for welfare homes, and allocating individual tenancies (i.e. of local authority houses)." Many committees approve all items of departmental expenditure, down to quite small amounts. There is often a reluctance to delegate matters to officials, attributed by the Maud Committee to the English tradition of local democracy which is "thought to imply that, unless the members determine how the smallest things are done, they are failing in their duties". It is also affected by the legal responsibility laid on the council as a whole. Some of the administrative effects of this concern are obviated by the informal relationship which often develops between the chairman of a committee and the chief officer of the department it supervises. The full committee can meet only relatively infrequently but administrative decisions have to be taken continuously—and the chairman and the chief officer can sometimes take them in the expectation of subsequent committee ratification. But there still often remains a whole range of matters, not all of major importance, which must wait on a committee decision.

The possible criteria for dividing up responsibilities between committees and departments are the same as those for allocating responsibilities between central government departments discussed in Chapter 3. On the whole in local government, as in Whitehall, the functional principle predominates. But since local committees and departments (unlike most Whitehall departments) are actually *providing* a service the functional principle at times seems more like a "work process" principle. Thus the senior officials of an education department are educationists, of a surveyor's department surveyors: senior local government officials, unlike their Whitehall counterparts, are "specialists" rather than "generalists". Some committees will in any case be explicitly organised on work process or "horizontal" lines in that they provide a common service for the whole authority, such as a works and building committee, an establishments committee, and (perhaps most importantly) a finance committee. The Maud Committee calculated that county and county borough councils had, on average, about twenty full committees (the largest authorities had up to thirty-five) and between forty and fifty sub-committees, together with a large number of *ad hoc* committees and sub-committees. This in itself obviously creates a tremendous task of co-ordination, especially in view of the concern of each full committee and the officials which serve it with a particular professional service. Some uniformity of practice is provided by the horizontal committees like those for finance, establishments, and "general purposes", or by joint co-ordinating committees or *ad hoc* meetings between members of different committees on matters of common concern. But probably the most significant part in the attempt to achieve some cohesion is played outside the formal committee structure—by the machinery of the local political parties and groups represented on the council.

Where the party system is most highly developed (for example, in the Greater London Council and in the councils of other big cities), something recognisably like a "Cabinet system" emerges, with members of the majority party monopolising the main committee chairmanships (as "*quasi*-ministers"), and with major council policy effectively determined, not in council and committee—in which members of the "opposition" party necessarily play a part—but in unofficial party group meetings, and backed by the sanctions of party discipline. But even in this situation the parallel with the Cabinet can never be exact. The party leaders on a local authority are unpaid and there is always a residuum of administrative or policy issues not involving "party lines" which can be considered by the appropriate committee—representing both or all the parties on the council—in a way impossible in central government, where opposition members are *ipso facto* excluded from governmental decision-making. But by no means all authorities *are* organised on party lines, and many of those which are, are very differently constituted from the normal two-party hegemony at Westminster—either having a number of party groups with no clear majority for one, or having one party in a dominant or even monopolistic position over a period of many years. It is impossible to be precise about the number of party-organised authorities since definitions and designations vary considerably (e.g.,

ratepayers, "independents"), but the research study commissioned by the Maud Committee recorded that, in a ques-
tionnaire sent to all authorities, those questions which had to
be answered by authorities operating on a party basis received replies from 31 per cent of the counties, 86 per cent of
the county boroughs, 45 per cent of the non-county boroughs,
43 per cent of the urban districts, and 8 per cent of the rural
districts (which all almost certainly represent an under-
estimate of the actual proportion) and all the London boroughs.

Officials too, concerned as they are with the day-to-day
administration of the local authority's work, have an obvious
part to play in co-ordination. But the chief officers are professionally qualified and might be expected to be more concerned with their own professional service than with the
needs of the authority as a whole. Thus the criticism sometimes made of the higher officials of local government is
almost the exact opposite of that made of the administrative
class of the Civil Service: the latter, it is argued, are too
amateur, local government officials, too professional.

The role of the clerk to the council has increasingly
been seen to be crucial in the attempt to co-ordinate the work
of a local authority, at least at the official level and also perhaps at the policy level. It has no parallel in central government unless the rather inappropriate analogy is drawn between
the various departments of a local authority and a *single*
government department—in which case the clerk becomes
a kind of permanent secretary. But the more realistic analogy
is with the whole range of central government departments
and here—despite the functions exercised by the Secretary
to the Cabinet and by the Head of the Home Civil Service
—there is no central official co-ordinator in the way a local
authority clerk may potentially be. The problem has always been that the clerk as such has no hierarchical superiority over the chief officers professionally responsible for their
own services and departments to the council and its appropriate committee. But by the nature of his work as legal
adviser to a body (the local council) which is circumscribed
by law, and his functions as the main point of contact for the
council and its committees (e.g., by the centralisation of

minutes in his office), and for the world outside the authority, even a clerk with a minimal view of his general co-ordinating role cannot avoid some co-ordinating functions.

The development of the idea of the clerk as co-ordinator goes back over forty years. The 1923–4 report of the Ministry of Health (at that time the department with general responsibility for local government) made reference to it, and in 1929 the Royal Commission on Local Government said in its report that it was imperative that one officer should be in a position to survey the whole field of the authority's activities and to secure co-ordination. It concluded that the most suitable officer was the clerk, recognising that his success would depend on his personality and on his relations with other chief officers (the commission did not go so far as to recommend that the clerk should be in executive control, able to give instructions to his fellow chief officers). Five years later (1934) the Hadow Committee on the recruitment, training, and promotion of local government officers reported in favour of regarding the clerk as the chief administrative officer of the council: "The council will look to him for advice on all major questions. He is the channel of their official correspondence, and responsible for the conduct of important negotiations on their behalf. The Clerk should co-ordinate the work of several departments, should keep in touch with the decisions of each of the committees, and should exercise a general supervision over all the work without interfering with heads of departments in strictly technical questions"; while he will normally be responsible for the legal business of the authority "his administrative functions are the more important". In 1949 the nationally-negotiated conditions of service for clerks echoed the Hadow Committee recommendation in stating that the clerk "shall be the chief executive and administrative officer of the council ... responsible for co-ordinating the whole work of the council", but there was no attempt to reconcile this with the conditions of service of other chief officers, under which they are responsible to the council through the appropriate committees—their relationship with the clerk is not defined. When the Treasury Organisation and Methods Division reported on Coventry city council reorganisation in 1953 it came out strongly in favour of the clerk being the chief administrative officer in the full sense, responsible for: securing economy in administration, inter-departmental co-ordination, establishment work, common office services, organisation and methods and oversight of the machinery for implementing policy decisions—a co-ordinator of executive action (but not of policy). Subsequently several authorities, notably Newcastle-upon-Tyne and Basildon, appointed clerks with over-riding co-ordinating functions (some of them without the legal qualifications traditional to clerks): in Newcastle he is called the Principal City Officer and in Basildon the Town Manager. The evidence given to the Maud Committee showed that there was no unanimity on the question for it ranged from advocacy of an official on the lines of the city manager in certain American cities or the manager of a commercial organisation, "who would formulate policy, co-ordinate its execution and also direct the authority's business" to the maintenance of the existing *status quo*, with the clerk something more than "first among equals".

In its recommendations on internal organisation in its report published in May 1967 the Maud Committee was particularly concerned with what it saw as the inherent tendency of local authority organisation to fragmentation: "The general conception is that of an assemblage of committees, each carrying out its own special duties and championing its own causes, with reliance on horizontal committees, personal contacts, party machinery, and the efforts of officers to achieve co-ordination". The committee made three main groups of recommendations on the role of the council and its committees:

1. There should be a clearer division of labour between council members and officers. Members must exercise sovereign power within the authority and accepted responsibility for everything done in the council's name. But having settled the policy they must delegate to officers the taking of all but the most important decisions.

2. Committees should cease to be executive or administrative, save for some exceptional purposes, and become

mainly deliberative. There should be as few committees as possible, perhaps not more than six even in large authorities. Each committee should concern itself with a group of subjects, e.g., a social work committee, dealing with child care, personal health and welfare. There should be as few sub-committees as possible.

3. A Management Board, with from between five and nine members (paid a part-time salary), should be appointed by all but the smallest authorities to serve as the focal point for the management of the authority's affairs and to supervise the work of the authority as a whole. It would be the sole channel through which business done in the committees reached the council. The board would itself formulate and present proposals requiring council approval. It would also propose the establishment and dis-establishment of committees. The full council would debate and decide questions put to it by the board, which would sometimes circulate before debate "white papers" on important policy issues. Full opportunity should also be given in council for members to ask questions and table motions for debate.

The Maud Committee envisaged that where the council was organised on political lines members of parties other than the majority party would be offered representation on the Management Board, thus enabling a knowledge of council business to be shared and ensuring a continuity of experience if there should be a change of party control. In this form the board could not, of course, be an ordinary "Cabinet" but might be a kind of "coalition" one. This recommendation, on the face of it, looks naive. In the light of the experience of party operation in local government the most likely development would seem either a monopoly of Management Board membership by the majority party or the continuance, alongside the formal multi-party Management Board, of informal party groups—that of the majority party making the effective policy decisions.

On the official side the Maud Committee (like the Mallaby Committee on staffing before it) recommended that each authority should appoint its clerk as undisputed

head of the official staff. He should not necessarily be a qualified lawyer but should be chosen for qualities of leadership
and for managerial ability. He would be the chief officer to
the Management Board. The other chief officers should form
a team under the clerk's leadership and report to the council
through him. The committee also recommended a stream-
lining of the departmental structure, with departments
grouped together under not more than about six chief
officers.

The Maud Committee considered that all the statutory
constraints on internal organisation (see p. 119) should be
removed. It believed that "No radical reform of the internal
organisation based on our view of the responsibilities of members and officers is possible under the present requirements of
the law". Thus it proposed the repeal of the statutory provisions requiring local authorities to establish certain
committees and those involving ministerial approval of the
appointment or dismissal of certain chief officers. To enable
discretion to be formally exercised by officials the committee
recommended that statutory recognition should be given to
the proposition that "Anything required and authorised
under an Act to be done by a local authority may be done by
an officer of the authority authorised in that behalf by the
authority either generally or specifically". It also recommended the abolition of the power of surcharge possessed by
the district auditor. (The Maud Committee's recommendations
were broadly endorsed by the subsequent Royal Commission
with the same chairman, under his new title of Lord Redcliffe-
Maud.)

Central-Local Relations

The relationship with central government is a crucial
one for local authorities. The doctrine of *ultra vires* compels
them to be able to point to statutory sanction—in general
enabling legislation, in specific legislation or in private Acts—
for every action taken by them. Recourse to Parliament for
statutory powers can only, for the most part, be made under
the aegis of a minister. A provision in the Local Government

Administration by Local Authorities

(Financial Provisions) Act of 1963 empowers local councils
to incur expenditure "for any purpose which in their opinion
is in the interests of their area or its inhabitants" and for
which no statutory power already exists. But such expenditure
must not exceed the product of a penny rate and it has not
materially altered the situation. The Maud Committee
proposed that local authorities should be given by statute a
general competence to do (in addition to what legislation
already requires or permits them to do) whatever in their
opinion is in the interests of their areas and their inhabitants
subject to their not encroaching on the duties of other governmental bodies and to appropriate safeguards for the protection
of public and private interests.

As we have seen, ministers usually have specific supervisory functions laid on them in statutes extending the
responsibilities of local authorities. These supervisory functions
can extend far beyond general policy to almost unbelievably
detailed matters of administration, of which the Maud Committee gives examples in its report. The Secretary of State
for Education and Science must authorise the removal of a
school to a new site; grievances from parents concerning
school attendance orders may be submitted to him and he may
give such directions as he sees fit; he must approve proposals
for the establishment of camps, holiday classes, and playing
fields at which facilities for recreation and social and physical
training are provided; he may direct a local authority to
provide transport facilities for pupils and may, by regulations,
empower local authorities to provide clothing suitable for
physical training. Similarly, the minister responsible for the
health services (now the Secretary of State for Social Services)
"must be satisfied about provision, equipment, staffing, and
maintenance of health centres. Arrangements for providing
domestic help for households when this is required, owing to
the presence of any person who is ill, lying-in, an expectant
mother, aged, or a child not over compulsory school age, must
be approved by the Minister."

But the main control is over general policy, above all
where local authorities are responsible for administering
services in which there is a general acceptance of the need

for a national minimum standard of provision—and this includes all the important functions like education, health and welfare services and planning. It is this control over the adequacy of the service provided by the local authority which "is at the heart of the whole relationship" (J. A. G. Griffith). As regards the local education authorities (counties and county boroughs), for example, the Secretary of State for Education and Science controls the school-building programme and prescribes the standards to which school premises are to conform; his approval is necessary for their educational development plans; he maintains a staff of inspectors to examine the working of the schools; and if he is satisfied that an authority is failing in its statutory duties he may give directions to enforce performance. But there are practical limitations on the enforcement of a policy by a central department. It was assumed by the education ministry (to continue the example of education) in the years immediately following the Education Act of 1944 that education authorities would provide three types of secondary schools, with selective entry at eleven plus (although the Act was silent on the matter). But apart from the beginning some authorities— London, Middlesex, Coventry, Oldham, and the West Riding, for example—decided to provide non-selective comprehensive secondary schools, while other authorities experimented with alternative methods of organising secondary education. At first widely unpopular, comprehensive schools later came to be seen as an effective method of obviating the generally-admitted inequalities of secondary selection at eleven plus. In the 1960s local education authorities began increasingly to seek to reorganise their secondary systems on comprehensive lines; but many retained the tri-partite system. Although for some time before the 1964 election the Conservative Government had ceased to oppose comprehensive schemes its super-session by a Labour Government brought a positive drive to secure the adoption of the comprehensive principle by all authorities. The new policy was enshrined in a 1965 departmental circular which requested authorities, if they had not already done so, to prepare and submit to the minister plans for reorganising secondary education in their areas on comprehensive lines, consulting as freely as possible with the department at all stages before submission of the plans. Most authorities subsequently produced schemes the department considered satisfactory, with or without amendment, but some remained obdurate, at any rate for a time. The whole process has revealed at least two facets of the central-local relationship:

(1) that national policy is often formulated in the light of experience gained in particular authorities rather than merely imposed by the central government, and

(2) that, in the last analysis, central government's activities in relation to local government, like those of local government itself, are controlled by statute—to *compel* an unwilling authority to adopt a comprehensive system requires new legislation.

In such cases central departments prefer to rely on persuasion or other less extreme methods, and there are a wide variety of influences and controls available to departments. Circulars are issued to obtain information, to explain new legislation, to introduce departmental publications, and to give policy or technical advice to local authorities. Ministers have appellate and confirmatory functions in the approval of proposals relating to certain services and for compulsory purchase and slum clearance orders; while they act in a *quasi*-judicial capacity in, for example, disputes between local education authorities and school governors. In addition to inspectors of schools there are police and fire inspectorates, all having both inspectorial and advisory duties. Other inspectors conduct inquiries into compulsory purchase and slum clearance orders, and into development plans and planning appeals (statutory inquiries will be dealt with in Chapter 8). Then there are the powers to act in default of a local authority which ministers have in respect to certain services, including libraries, housing, and planning—rarely used, but sometimes effective as a damoclean sword held over the head of recalcitrant authorities.

But the most dramatic evidence of the twentieth century dependence of local authorities on central government is in the field of finance. Apart from receipts from housing rents and trading services (the net amount of which is not of great importance overall) the one major source of local revenue entirely within local authority control—the rates levied on occupiers of land and buildings—has proved increasingly inadequate to finance the expanding responsibilities placed on local authorities, especially highly expensive social services like education. The result has been a growing dependence on central government grants: whereas in 1914 government grants accounted for about 25 per cent of total local authority expenditure they now account for over 50 per cent. While it may be true that there is no logical link between increasing central government financial help and central government control (which may in any case be necessary even when the whole cost is borne locally), in practice it seems to have this effect, and at the very least local authority financial dependence adds to the sanctions available to central government (e.g., a threat to withhold a grant). The pattern of revenue grants from central government to local authorities has been a complicated and ever-changing one. The expedients have been many: grants for specific services, either on a percentage or lump-sum basis, the short-lived "assigned revenues" of 1888 (e.g., from the national alcohol duties), "block" or general grants for a range of services, grants to mitigate the effects of varying rateable values per head of population. It has sometimes been claimed that an emphasis on block or general grants (like that which was in operation for some years under the Local Government Act of 1958) rather than on specific grants increases the independence of local authorities in the spending of their money, but there is no evidence for this: the various individual elements within a general grant seem to be as tightly controlled by the appropriate government departments as if they were separate grants for a single service.

The regressive nature of rates, which are onerous for poorer households, has militated against a full utilisation of this administratively convenient and indubitably local form of taxation. The central government has increasingly limited local government's freedom in levying rates. In 1948 it took over responsibility for the valuation of rateable values and with it the decision as to how far it should reflect rising property values (until 1963 assessments for rateable purposes were based on 1939 property values and although five-yearly valuations on current values were provided for thereafter the central government is free to postpone a revaluation—as it did the one due in 1968). In 1966 the government took statutory powers to mitigate the effects of rate increases by transferring part of them to national taxation. The Rating Act of 1966 (in addition to providing rate rebates for rate-payers of limited means) has entirely recast central-local relations on the revenue side. A new rate support grant has become the main channel of central government aid to the major local authorities—counties, county boroughs, and London boroughs—accounting for something like 90 per cent of the total grant (leaving specific grants still payable, for example, for police and housing). The major part of the rate support grant is distributed to local authorities on the basis of population, numbers of pupils and students and other factors affecting expenditure needs; another part is distributed to all authorities with below average rate resources, as with the previous rate deficiency grant; and the remaining part is applied in the reduction of the rates levied on domestic ratepayers. The Maud Committee saw significance in the fact that the new arrangements had been designed to allow the central government for the first time to influence expenditure on all local authority services.

The 1966 Act was intended as an interim measure pending a major reform of local government finance, including consideration of possible alternatives to rates as a source of local revenue, which could only be undertaken after the royal commissions on local government in England and Scotland, appointed in 1966, had completed their work. It is difficult to see what shape the reform can take. Whatever their defects, rates are a flexible source of revenue and most of the suggested alternatives—such as a return to "assigned revenues" in the form of motor vehicles duties, for example—would not provide for increases at the decision of local authorities rather than central government, while revenue from a local income or sales tax would, unlike that from rates, be unpredictable. On present trends it looks as if the flexible element will be the government grant but as Griffith has observed, "If grant monies are to become this element, with rate income in effect frozen at a particular level, then the independence of local authorities is indeed threatened" (*Central Departments and Local Authorities*). The Redcliffe-Maud Report of 1969 also stressed that "a reasonable measure of financial independence is an essential element in local democracy" and, while recommending that new sources of local revenue should be made available to local authorities, expressed the belief that rates would remain the chief local tax.

Central control over local authority borrowing for *capital* expenditure is even greater than that over its revenue expenditure. Capital expenditure, such as the cost of building a school (as opposed to revenue or current expenditure such as the cost of *running* a school), cannot be met out of the income of a single year and is for the most part financed by borrowing, loans being repaid with interest out of the revenue of succeeding years. Local authorities borrow either through the Treasury-financed Public Works Loan Board or direct from the public in the form of mortgages or stock issues. Under the Local Government Act of 1933 local authorities have a general power to borrow for the purposes of acquiring land, erecting buildings, executing any permanent work or any other project for which they are statutorily authorised to borrow, but nevertheless its exercise is subject to permission from the Minister of Housing and Local Government (in Scotland and Wales, their respective Secretaries of State) or for a few purposes, the Minister of Transport. This takes the form of a loan sanction which is issued only after detailed scrutiny, to which even the largest authorities are subject (the Greater London Council, however, obtains borrowing powers by annual statute). Central control of borrowing was originally instituted to prevent local authorities from undertaking commitments beyond their means. It is now employed (as with the nationalised industries) for the purposes of controlling the national economy, by ensuring that local government investment programmes are in line with the national programme and the existing financial situation. The Maud Committee suggested that this control might be effected more easily and with less control over details by the use of block sanctions, designed to allow local authorities more latitude in the choice of projects.

A further reason for the extent and detailed nature of central control lies in the diversity of population, areas and— intimately linked with the other two—resources possessed by local authorities with the same formal status and, in general, the same powers. This is partly the result of the Victorian structure of local government outside Greater London, con- sisting of administrative counties, within them second-tier county districts (non-county boroughs, urban and rural districts) and, outside their jurisdiction, the single-tier county boroughs. Since the reforms of 1888–94 which gave rise to this structure there have been vast changes in the distribution and mobility of the population induced by the revolution in communications, in the scope and nature of local authority functions, in central-local relations, in administrative prac- tices, and in public attitudes. Population movements, in particular, have aggravated disparities of population and resources. It is difficult to distribute functions rationally when counties may vary in population from 30,000 to $2\frac{1}{2}$ million and county boroughs from 30,000 to over 1 million, and when a half of all authorities (other than the parishes into which rural districts are divided) have populations of less than 20,000. An education authority with a population of 50,000 obviously cannot provide the services and specialist staff possible for an authority of 500,000, even though it may be just as administratively efficient within its smaller means. Joint arrangements between neighbouring authorities (joint committees are in any case normal for police and water authorities) may mitigate some of the effects but cannot provide a long-term solution. The effect on central attitudes can be two-fold. First, there may be a tendency to remove functions from local government or not to give it functions which might have been devolved on it had the structure been more rational. Since 1946 local government as a whole has lost responsibilities for trunk roads, rating valuation, hospitals, electricity and gas undertakings, and public assis- tance, while its role in functions of great local importance—

including regional planning, traffic and higher education—
has been diminishing. The other effect is to lead to the determination of the extent of central control by the needs of the
weakest authorities, thus subjecting larger authorities to
unnecessarily detailed supervision.

It would not be appropriate here to recount all the various
reform proposals (in which the local government associations
have played a major part) put forward from the Local
Government Boundary Commission of 1945–9 onwards. Major
changes were effected in the Greater London area (with a
population of over 8 million) in 1965 when, following the
Herbert Royal Commission Report of 1960 and the subsequent
legislation, a congeries of over 100 local authorities was replaced by a Greater London Council, responsible for functions
requiring the largest possible "catchment areas" (e.g.,
major planning development, metropolitan roads and traffic,
sewage, fire and ambulance services), with thirty-two London
boroughs, and the City of London, to provide the main
personal services. In the rest of England several changes have
been made as a result of the reports of the Local Government
Commission from 1959 to its abolition in 1966, but all have
been within the existing county-county borough structure, as
are the changes proposed in the 1967 government White
Paper on local government in Wales (apart from the creation
of a nominated Council for Wales with, however, no executive
responsibilities). A Royal Commission for England (together
with one for Scotland) was created in 1966 to formulate
the principles on which a reformed structure might be based.

The English (Redcliffe-Maud) Commission published
its report in June 1969 and the government immediately
announced its acceptance "in principle" of its recommendations. The report proposed the replacement of the 1,210
authorities in England outside London by eighty-one new
authorities: fifty-eight single-tier or unitary authorities with
populations ranging from about 250,000 to one million and
a two-tier system (on the Greater London model) in the three
conurbations of Birmingham, Liverpool, and Manchester.
For certan broad planning functions the eighty-one authorities, together with the existing thirty-four authorities in

Greater London, would be grouped into eight provinces, roughly corresponding in area to the economic planning regions. The authorities which the new arrangements would supersede would maintain a continued existence as "local councils" but without statutory powers as such; they would, however, be able to provide certain local amenities and act as representatives of local opinion.

The expectation is that fewer and larger authorities will reduce the extent of central control, although there seems no necessary reason why this should be so. But at least stronger authorities could lead to that control being more concerned with broad strategy and less with detailed administration. The Redcliffe-Maud Report indeed envisaged that as soon as local government was reorganised government departments concerned with local government "should be required to review . . . every point at which they control or regulate the actions of authorities. All rules or regulations, all requirements for consent or approval, which have no demonstrable value under the new local government system should be repealed."

It is in a sense misleading to talk of central government control of local authorities. In the first place, many policy initiatives have originated from the authorities themselves. The relationship is thus very much a two-way process, with a great deal of the dialogue on the local authority side being conducted through the local government associations (especially the Association of Municipal Corporations, representing both non-county and county boroughs, and the County Councils Association). J. A. G. Griffith has commented that it would be difficult to exaggerate the importance of the local authority associations in influencing legislation, governmental policies, and administration and in acting as co-ordinators and channels of local authority opinion: they provide, indeed, a classic example of interest group politics (see Chapter 7). Nevertheless, the normal day-to-day relationship between government departments and local authorities is a direct one.

Secondly, "central government" is, in this context, central government *departments*, each concerned primarily with the particular function for which it is responsible. Each

local authority, however, is *multi*-functional and has to deal
with a variety of departments, none of them really interested
in the work of local government as a whole. The Ministry
of Housing and Local Government, it is true, has some important general functions (e.g., loan sanction, district audit), but
it is essentially the central ministry responsible for a number
(but by no means all) of the major local government functions—notably public health, housing, and town and country
planning. Each department, Griffith has shown, has its own
attitude to local government which distinguishes it from other
departments, and there are even differences between sections
responsible for a particular local authority function in the same
department (e.g., the Children's and Police departments of
the Home Office). Griffith differentiates between three types
of departmental attitude: (1) the *laissez-faire* (i.e., "not a
negative attitude of indifference but a positive philosophy of
as little interference as possible"), which characterised the
Ministry of Health on both its health and welfare sides; (2) the
regulatory, typified by the Home Office in relation to the children's services; and (3) the *promotional*, of which the Department
of Education and Science is perhaps the most notable example.
The analysis is, of course, a very rough one, and elements of
each attitude may be seen in the supervision of one service by
one department. As regards housing, for example, the attitude
of the Ministry of Housing and Local Government is *laissez-
faire* in that it leaves local housing authorities to determine
housing needs and the extent to which they should be met;
regulatory, in its control of standards, lay-out, and design; and
promotional, in the volume of advisory material issued and
departmental sponsorship of local authority building con-
sortia. To some extent the functional division in Whitehall is
matched in the departmental organisation of local authorities.
There is a good deal of dialogue between chief officers in
local authorities (especially the larger authorities) and their
professional opposite numbers in Whitehall, both concerned,
as they are, with their particular specialism, whether it be
education or road-building. This sometimes leads to a tendency, commented on by the Maud Committee, for the local
authority service committees and their chief officers to look

primarily to central departments to sanction their projects rather than a directing body in their own authority. Thus the fragmentation which the Maud Committee deplored in the local authority system is accentuated because of the lack of co-ordination between government departments. It was with this in mind that it included in its report the recommendation that "the Government should consider setting up an enquiry in the hope that it may be found possible to appoint a single Minister who would be responsible for co-ordinating the policy of the central government in so far as it bears on the functions of local authorities". This would be paralleled on the local authority side by a Local Government Central Office which would, among other things, review in collaboration with central government the powers of local authorities and the administrative controls exerted by departments; carry out research into local government services and the internal organisation of local authorities; and operate a central local authority staffing and staff training organisation.

Finally, it has to be remembered that although the central government is clearly dominant in the central-local "partner-ship" the relationship is still one of mutual interdependence. The point is well made by the Redcliffe-Maud Report, in the context of its radical proposals for local government reform. "The close involvement of the national government in the affairs of local government is, today, inescapable (the report says). We believe, however, that this only increases the need for strong and independent-minded local authorities, speaking with a voice to which the national government must listen, capable of injecting their ideas into national policies, competent to implement the policies in whatever way is best suited to local conditions, and without the need for any detailed supervision. It is the fact that so much is now asked of local government that is in part responsible for the increased involvement of Whitehall. The reverse side of the coin is that central government has become increasingly dependent on local authorities. Ministers cannot secure the results they want —whether better housing, better education, better health and welfare services, modernisation of the environment, management of transportation—except by means of fully competent authorities, able both to play their part, from their local knowledge, in the development of policies, and to exercise an independent judgement in deciding how the policies can best be applied, and social needs can best be met, in their particular conditions."

For Further Reading

"Allen Report"—*Report of the Committee of Inquiry into the Impact of Rates on Households* (Cmnd. 2582, H.M.S.O., 1965).

Brand, J. A., "Ministry Control and Local Autonomy in Education" in *Political Quarterly*, 36 (1965), 154–63.

Bulpitt, J. G., *Party Politics in English Local Government* (Longmans, 1967).

Chester, D. N., "Local Democracy and the Internal Organisation of Local Authorities" in *Public Administration*, 46 (1968), 287–98.

Gowan, Ivor, and Gibson, Leon, "The Royal Commission on Local Government in England" in *Public Administration*, 46 (1968), 13–24.

Griffith, J. A. G., *Central Departments and Local Authorities* (Allen & Unwin, 1966).

Headrick, T. E., *The Town Clerk in English Local Government* (Allen & Unwin, 1962).

"Herbert Report"—*Report of the Royal Commission on Local Government in Greater London 1957–60* (Cmnd. 1164, H.M.S.O., 1960).

Jackson, R. M., *The Machinery of Local Government* (Macmillan, 2nd edn., 1965).

Jennings, Sir Ivor, *Principles of Local Government Law* (University of London Press, 4th edn. by J. A. G. Griffith, 1960).

Maddick, H., and Pritchard, E. P., "The Conventions of Local Government in the West Midlands" in *Public Administration*, 36 (1958), 145–56 and 37 (1959), 135–44.

"Mallaby Report"—*Report of the Committee on Staffing of Local Government* (H.M.S.O., 1967).

Maud, Sir J., and Finer, S. E., *Local Government in England and Wales* (Oxford U.P., 1953).

"Maud Report"—Vol. 1: *Report of the Committee on Management of Local Government* (H.M.S.O., 1967).

—Vol. 5: *Local Government Administration in England and Wales* (An Enquiry carried out for the Committee) (H.M.S.O., 1967).

"Redcliffe-Maud Report"—*Report of the Royal Commission on Local Government in England 1966–1969* (Cmnd. 4040, H.M.S.O., 3 vols., 1969). (Various research studies, written evidence and minutes of evidence published separately.)

Richards, P. G., *The New Local Government System* (Allen & Unwin, 1968).

Royal Institute of Public Administration, *Management of Local Government: The Maud Committee Report* (Report of a Conference 12–13 December, 1967) (R.I.P.A., 1968).

Sharp, E., *The Ministry of Housing and Local Government* (Allen & Unwin, 1969).

Smellie, K. B., *A History of Local Government* (Allen & Unwin, 4th edn., 1968).

Stanyer, J., *County Government in England and Wales* (Routledge & Kegan
    Paul, 1967).
Steer, William S., "Local Government" in Wiseman, H. Victor (ed.),
    Political Science (Routledge & Kegan Paul, 1967).
West Midland Study Group, *Local Government and Central Control* (Routledge
    & Kegan Paul, 1956).
Wiseman, H. Victor, *Local Government at Work* (Routledge & Kegan Paul,
    1967).

7. Public Accountability: Parliament and Organised Publics

Public administration necessarily exists to serve the public and "the criterion of its excellence is that it should give good service subject to public control" (Mackenzie and Grove). Service and control are clearly linked since, in the last analysis, it is only the public served by the administration which can determine the quality and effectiveness of the service provided. As a result of the "administrative revolution" of the twentieth century, notably in the vast expansion of public social services and of government involvement in the nation's economic life, members of the public now confront the administrative machinery of the State at many points in their everyday life. The State (to quote the Fulton Report) "taxes them and determines their rights to social benefits; it provides for the education of their children and the protection of their families' health. As householders, many are dependent on the State's housing policies; as employers and employees, they are deeply affected by its success or failure in the management of the national economy. In practice, most people can discharge many of their obligations to their families only with the help of the services provided and controlled by the State." Public administrators are thus "bound constantly to touch very sensitive nerves", in a way which has no parallel with the task of administration in private industry or commerce, for example. But much of the work of public administration is of a technicality and complexity beyond the understanding of most citizens who are, in any case, naturally more concerned with their individually-conceived needs than with "the public interest" which is (or should be) the concern of public administration. There can be no simple means of ensuring public accountability: there are a variety of ways in which public administrators have to answer for their activities. Many doubt whether, in total, they constitute adequate accountability, while others argue that, in addition to failing to secure effective accountability, they often positively militate against efficient administration. The question as to how far accountability can be reconciled with efficiency is unresolved: probably the best that can be hoped for is a rough equilibrium between the two. All that is attempted in this and the following chapter is a review of some of the main avenues through which the quest for accountability has been pursued.

Parliament

The main control of public administration is, of course, political. The administrative machinery is headed by ministers, who, in normal circumstances, are leading members of the majority party in the House of Commons and as such collectively responsible to the House and, through it, to the electorate. But, as has been frequently pointed out, this ministerial responsibility is fundamentally affected by the nature of the British political system. Party discipline ensures that ministers will be sustained by their party supporters on major policy issues (although, of course, the formulation of those policies may well have been affected by pressures from the government backbenchers in party meetings). And even when, on those rare occasions in this century when governments have not had an overall majority in the Commons (i.e., 1924 and 1929–31), Parliament has been able to "control" the government in the sense of the ability to engineer its downfall, this control was exercised, not by some autonomous arbitral institution, but by parties and groups with their own partisan interests. Elections obviously play their part in changing the personnel constituting the political leadership of the administration but they are too infrequent and too generalised in their nature to provide an effective check on the detailed operations of the machinery of administration.

Ministers at the head of government departments have an individual responsibility to Parliament as well as being subsumed under the collective responsibility of the government as a whole. Much of parliamentary procedure revolves around this individual ministerial responsibility since it is the responsible minister (or a junior minister on his behalf) who answers questions about the work of his department, introduces legislation within its field of activity and so on. But the responsibility, or rather, "answerability", does not mean that the minister is subject to the *control* of Parliament in any practical sense. Parliament (effectively the House of Commons) is here again not an arbitral body but one whose members are linked to the government—or opposed to it— by party ties. S. E. Finer has clearly demonstrated that there is no parliamentary sanction against a departmental minister apart from pressures within the government party. The widely-held belief that there is a firm convention of ministerial resignation in the face of a sustained attack on the conduct of a minister or his department is simply not borne out by the facts, unless the minister's own party wishes to see him go (and even this may be withstood if the Prime Minister and Cabinet are intent on retaining their colleague and make it a matter of *collective* responsibility). There are indeed several precedents for resignation by ministers on grounds of personal acts, both those which had no policy implications (e.g., Thomas in 1936, Dalton in 1947, Profumo in 1963) and those which did involve policy which the Cabinet repudiated (e.g., Seely in 1914, Montagu in 1922, Hoare in 1935). But *vicarious* resignations—that is, resignations arising from the acts of civil servants within a minister's department (and it is these which are much the more important from the point of view of controlling the administration)—have been relatively few. Some have arisen from what many considered to be the abnormally austere code of conduct of the minister concerned (e.g., Austen Chamberlain in 1917). The "classic" case was the resignation of Sir Thomas Dugdale as Minister of Agriculture in 1954 over the actions of his officials in the disposal of previously-requisitioned land at Crichel Down in Dorset, but even here it has been argued that it was the minister's sense of duty rather than the needs of the situation which led to his resignation.

The doctrine of vicarious ministerial responsibility (with or without the sanction of resignation) runs in double harness with that of the political anonymity of civil servants. The fact that it is the temporary political heads who answer in public for their departments is held to guarantee the continuance of a permanent, non-partisan Civil Service. But the interdependence of the two doctrines is now widely questioned. Ministers, briefed by civil servants who monopolise most of the relevant information about departmental activities, are thought by many to act as buffers rather than sources of genuine insights into the administrative process. The nature of the work of modern departments in any case makes it imposssible for a minister to have full detailed knowledge and control of all the activities of his officials. Civil servants are not immune from public criticism (the officials involved in the Crichel Down affair, for example, were named and the nature of the disciplinary action against them disclosed). One authority (Bernard Crick) has claimed that, in practice, the ministerial responsibility which ministers adhere to means, first, "that no one else can control the actions of their civil servants" and second, "that they are not to be blamed if they can't themselves"; while another (Brian Chapman) sees the doctrine as the "principal reason why the British have been so reluctant to rationalise administrative institutions and to improve ministerial control". In such circumstances the answerability of ministers seems neither an adequate nor an appropriate vehicle for administrative scrutiny—and the sanction of resignation (if it exists) appears almost totally irrelevant.

The machinery available to the House of Commons for questioning the administration consists essentially of debates, parliamentary questions, and committees. The major debates are concerned with policy issues in which the attitudes and programmes of the major parties are engaged: they take place against a background of the "continuous election campaign" which Crick sees as the main activity of the House of Commons. Some debates raise detailed points of administration, particularly the short adjournment debates initiated by private members at the end of each day's proceedings in the Commons, but they hardly constitute a continuous parliamentary oversight of administrative activity. Question hour on each of the first four days of the parliamentary week ranges more widely but time is short and the questions are often more directed to the scoring of political points than the eliciting of significant information about executive action (although the Crichel Down affair, which first came into prominence as a result of a parliamentary question, is a notable exception). There is, moreover, a procedural limitation on the kind of question which can be asked. Ministers can be questioned only on matters which come within their formal ministerial responsibility and this can be interpreted very narrowly. The official acts of his civil servants certainly come within a minister's responsibility but not, if he is responsible for a nationalised industry, for example, matters of day-to-day administration in that industry. The restriction on questions about the nationalised industries has been a permanent source of disquiet among backbenchers but despite various reformulations of the position in 1948, 1960, and 1963 there is still a major difference of scope between the parliamentary questions which can be asked of a minister about his government department and those which can be asked about a nationalised industry which he supervises. Departments undoubtedly give a high priority to seeking answers to satisfy parliamentary questioners but it must be doubted whether the expenditure of administrative effort is always justified by the amount of real democratic control secured. A member's question may often be answered more satisfactorily if less dramatically by means of a question for written rather than oral answer (and which are not circumscribed by the limits of the parliamentary question hour) or—perhaps most effectively—by direct approach to the department. But the problem remains of whether ordinary members are in a position to ask the vital questions of the administration—of whether in fact they are informed enough to know what information to seek. And it is here that the device of the specialist select committee is thought by its many advocates to have an important role to play.

Like other legislative bodies the House of Commons makes use of committees to assist it in its main functions of debating and voting on the legislation, policies, and activities of the government. But unlike many other legislatures (and local councils) none of these committees has executive powers, apart from committees administering aspects of the House's domestic business (e.g., the House of Commons Services Committee and its various sub-committees). Moreover, the composition of the committees reflects voting strengths in the House as a whole and in so far as they deal with matters of inter-party controversy (which is not often) the party system operates in them as it does in the chamber. For certain matters the House (minus the Speaker) constitutes itself as a "Committee of the Whole", but this is of only procedural importance. Thus until 1967 the committee stage of the Finance Bill (i.e., the government revenue proposals) was always taken in the "Committee of Ways and Means", while the estimates of government expenditure were formally considered in "Committee of Supply". But both the Finance Bill and the estimates represent government policy and, as such, are hardly likely to be materially altered (other than with the consent of the government) by a body which reflects the government's majority. Commons' control of the government's financial policy, despite a procedural uniqueness which stems from its historical basis in the seventeenth century constitutional struggles between King and Parliament, is no greater than that over any other aspect of government policy. And the House's conventions reflect this: for long "Supply Days"—discussions on departmental estimates—have provided an opportunity for the opposition to choose the subjects for general policy debates, and now even the necessity of a tenuous formal link with the actual estimates (e.g., a debate on education would nominally derive from a consideration of the education estimates) has been dropped.

Commons' Select Committees

Commons' committees in the real sense are of two basic types: permanent *standing* committees to deal with the committee stage of legislation, and *ad hoc* or permanent *select* committees to investigate specific matters. The standing committees are not specialised (with the partial exception of the Scottish standing committee) and are essentially deliberative and legislative bodies, behaving rather like microcosms of the House in that decisions are taken by voting on party lines. Much more important from the point of view of administrative scrutiny are the select committees, which include two committees concerned with finance—the Public Accounts Committee, first set up in 1861, and the Select Committee on Estimates, first set up in 1912—the Select Committee on Statutory Instruments (from 1944), and the Select Committee on Nationalised Industries (Reports and Accounts), first established in its present form at the end on 1956. Each of these committees has an element of specialisation and it would be appropriate to consider them briefly before going on to examine the extension of specialist committees as a means of assisting the Commons in its role of scrutinising the administration.

The Public Accounts Committee, with fourteen members and (unusual among Commons' committees) chaired by a member of the opposition, examines the annual accounts of government departments and the reports on them by the Comptroller and Auditor General, a parliamentary official, and his staff. Successive committees have come to interpret their rather limited terms of reference to cover investigations of whether full value has been obtained for the sums spent by departments and of cases in which the administration appears to have been faulty or negligent. The committee has thus become a powerful instrument for examining administrative activity, and has benefited from the expert assistance of the Comptroller and Auditor General, who has usually had previous high-level experience in the Treasury and is well versed in the ways of Whitehall. But the committee's *raison d'etre* is past expenditure, and it is this which has enabled it to exercise such influence on departmental practice—for past expenditure by definition represents administration, not policy. It questions civil servants (especially permanent secretaries in their capacity as accounting officers for their departments), not ministers. But the committee's reports can influence future practice, as when its 1964 report on the excessive profits gained by an electronics firm in supplying "Bloodhound" guided missiles to the (then) Ministry of Aviation led to a re-examination of departmental procedure for the costing of government contracts placed with outside firms. Probably no parliamentary body digs as deep into the administrative process as the Public Accounts Committee, although only a few accounts can be examined each year. There are indeed some who believe that its activities may sometimes in fact be harmful to the efficiency of administration by inducing a play-safe and negative attitude among civil servants and thus creating a kind of "negative efficiency audit" (the Fulton Committee believed that such an outlook militated against their principle of "accountable management" in the Civil Service, referred to above, p. 83). But if the Public Accounts Committee is to be regarded as a case study of the role of a parliamentary investigating committee then perhaps its most significant feature is that votes are rarely taken and party politics rarely obtrude. Thus it was a committee with a Conservative majority which produced the report on the "Bloodhound" missile contract criticising a department headed by a Conservative minister.

The main functions of the Select Committee on Estimates are to examine departmental estimates for the current year and to report how, if at all, the policy implied in them can be carried out more economically. With over thirty members it is the largest of the permanent select committees but it always works through sub-committees, each taking particular estimates. In practice the committee reports have no effect on current estimates (which have in any case usually been passed by Parliament before any report is submitted) but, like those of the Public Accounts Committee, they can influence future practice. Like the Public Accounts Committee, too, the Estimates Committee has interpreted its terms of reference widely and carries out, in a similarly non-partisan way, extensive investigations of the departments and their staffs under consideration. This was summed up in 1965 by the Head of the Home Civil Service as substituting for the question "Could this be done more cheaply?" the questions "Is value for money being obtained from this expenditure? Are the managerial arrangements under which this expenditure takes place fully effective? Does one get as good results as could be expected?" The Estimates Committee has had a harder task to establish itself than the Public Accounts Committee, largely because it is nominally dealing with estimates or present policy rather than with expenditure and past policy—but it has now become almost as important a tool of investigation as the older committee. It was, for example, a report from the Estimates Committee which led to the establishment of the Plowden Committee on public expenditure, while another report led to the setting up of the Fulton Committee on the Civil Service. Since 1965 an element of specialisation has been introduced into its work and most of its sub-committees now always deal with the same group of departmental estimates. Although it does not have the expert staff which the Public Accounts Committee possesses in the Comptroller and Auditor General and his department, the Estimates Committee now has power to employ advisers and assessors to assist on a particular enquiry.

The Select Committee on Statutory Instruments (informally known as the "Scrutiny Committee") has a much more limited function than the other select committees but its work does nevertheless impinge directly on aspects of the work of almost every government department. It was originally set up in 1944 (its establishment having been recommended by the Committee on Ministers' Powers in 1932) to provide the Commons with machinery to supervise the making of subordinate legislation by government departments under powers delegated to them, or rather to their minister, by "parent Acts". It would not be appropriate here to attempt to describe the highly complicated parliamentary procedure for the laying and approval or annulment of statutory instruments (which the Statutory Instruments Act of 1946 attempted, not altogether successfully, to clarify). All statutory instruments, like the legislation which empowers departments to make them, are made on the authority of the government, and the government's majority is invoked to defend them. Moreover, with an average of over 2,000 instruments submitted to Parliament each year it is not possible, in the press of business, to scrutinise even a very small proportion of them on the floor of the House. Within circumscribed terms of reference, which exclude it from considering the merits of particular instruments, the Scrutiny Committee (with an opposition member as chairman) has the task of examining instruments in draft and drawing the attention of the House to any which, for example, appear to "make some unusual or unexpected use of the powers conferred by the parent statute", exclude challenge in the courts, have been unjustifiably delayed in publication, or are "obscure in purport". Statistically its record is not impressive—in the eight years from 1957 to 1965 it reported on only thirty-six of the 5,171 instruments examined—but its usefulness is not really to be gauged from statistics. The committee's main influence is exercised through direct contact with departments, which often consult it in the actual process of drafting instruments. Once an instrument has appeared the committee can demand from the department concerned, often by taking evidence from the civil servants personally involved, explanations of delays in publication, or of obscurities in phrasing, or of lack of appropriate reference to the parent statute; in its investigations the committee has the expert legal assistance of the Speaker's Counsel. Thus its value is to be found not so much in the number of adverse reports it submits to the House as in the improvements in departmental practice and procedure for the framing of instruments which its efforts have secured.

The Select Committee on Nationalised Industries essentially originated from backbenchers' dissatisfaction with the limitations imposed on the asking of parliamentary questions on the activities of the industries. In December 1951 (soon after the first post-war Conservative government took office) an *ad hoc* select committee was appointed "to consider the present methods by which the House of Commons is informed of the nationalised industries and to report what changes, having regard to the provisions laid down by Parliament in the relevant statutes, may be desirable in these methods". In 1953 it reported that a permanent select committee should be appointed, assisted by an officer "of the status of the Comptroller and Auditor General" to keep the industries under continuous review. The government decided to set up such a committee, without the official assistance recommended, to examine the industries' reports and accounts, but forbade it to consider matters that were the responsibility of ministers, concerned wages or conditions of employment, were dealt with through formal machinery such as consumers' councils, or were concerned with day-to-day administration. The committee was first established in March 1955 but by November of the same year it reported that its terms of reference left it insufficient scope "to obtain further information which would be of any real use to the House". A year later another select committee was appointed, without the restrictive terms of reference, to examine the industries' reports and accounts, and it has been appointed for each subsequent parliamentary session. Perhaps rather surprisingly in view of the experience of its predecessors it quickly established itself as a valuable source of information about nationalised industries and, in particular, has provided extensive documentation on the minister-board relationship (see Chapter 5). Many consider it almost the archetype of a Commons' investigation committee, and one of the aims of a detailed academic study of its activities (by David Coombes) was "to demonstrate that specialised committees of this kind could be used, not only to look into the affairs of public corporations, but also to scrutinise the work of government departments". Coombes argues that the committee has not only added much to the public accountability of the nationalised industries but has shown how a committee with a specialised field of investigation can deal (1) with controversial issues in a non-partisan way (and nationalisation has been one

of the most controversial of post-war party political issues);
(2) with matters involving difficult constitutional and administrative considerations (e.g., the autonomous position of the
boards and the commercial character of the undertakings);
and (3) with government departments (i.e., those responsible
for nationalised industries) on questions of ministerial policy.

An extended use of specialist committees in the Commons has been advocated for many years, at least as far
back as the evidence of F. W. Jowett and Lloyd George to
the Commons' Select Committee on Procedure in 1931–2.
Some proposals (like Jowett's) have been designed to subvert
the Cabinet system by giving the Commons effective control
over executive activity; others, more realistic, have varied
between specialist committees for the second reading or
committee stages of legislation, for estimates or for departmental investigations—or for all these purposes together (it
is not always clear precisely what is being advocated by a
particular proponent). In recent years interest has centred
on the device of investigating committees, with the aim of
providing new channels of information about the activities
of government and new means of generating ideas about
future policy. It is argued that as long as there is an effective
opposition, major government policy decisions can be chal-
lenged within the traditional procedures of the Commons.
But these procedures are much less effective for the scrutiny
of how policies are administered. Question hour provides a
searching public examination of ministers but is an inadequate
method of elucidating the essential facts by which the efficiency
of administration can be judged; and general debates do
not provide an opportunity for detailed examination of
departmental activities. The Public Accounts, Estimates, and
Nationalised Industries Committees have shown the way
but their work has been primarily concerned with finance,
and the scope of administrative investigation needs to be
widened. The response of most party leaders, both those in
opposition and in government, to such advocacy was essentially that specialist committees would conflict with the
doctrine of ministerial responsibility because they would
(like U.S. congressional committees) be irresistibly tempted

to seek to control government policy and would, in any case, impose an intolerable burden on ministers. On the other side, it was argued that in the British system the government fully controls the Commons through the party unity of the majority party and that no subordinate committee would be allowed to interfere directly in policy. In any case, the important distinction is not that between "policy", in the sense of general matters, and "administration", in the sense of details, but the functional distinction between party issues— questions on which political parties are opposed (and on which party discipline is decisive)—and non-party issues, questions—whether general or detailed—on which members could find agreement irrespective of their party affiliations. Moreover, since the committees would be subordinate and advisory, they need not make excessive demands on ministers. Their main work (as with the financial committees) would be with officials and ministers would need to appear only occasionally to answer on controversial points or to sound the committee on general policy.

Little progress was made with the idea until the 1965 report of the Select Committee on Procedure. The committee had been much impressed with the evidence given to it on behalf of the Study of Parliament Group (consisting mainly of academic authorities under the chairmanship of a former Clerk to the House of Commons). Starting from the premise that "parliamentary control means influence, not direct power, advice, not command, criticism, not obstruction, scrutiny, not initiative, and publicity, not secrecy" (Crick, *Reform of Parliament*) the group concluded that the Commons could be assisted in regaining this kind of influence by a wider and more specialised use of select committees. Eventually the whole field of governmental activity might be divided into sections, each section being kept under observation by committees charged "to examine the assumptions on which policy decisions have been made and to report on the implementation of policy".

The Procedure Committee's own proposals were more modest than this but marked a significant advance on those of any of their predecessors (the 1959 committee, for example, had contented itself with discussing but finally rejecting the idea of a committee on colonial affairs). The committee came to the conclusion that, to help in the examination of government spending and administration, more information should be made available to M.P.s about the way government departments carried out their responsibilities so that when taking part in major Commons' debates on controversial issues they might be armed with the necessary background knowledge. This required a more efficient system of administrative scrutiny. The committee therefore recommended that a new select committee should be developed from the Estimates Committee and that it should work through about six specialist sub-committees to examine how departments discharged their responsibilities and to consider their estimates and reports. This, the committee felt, would satisfy both the need for investigation of long-term proposals for expenditure in various fields and for an examination of administrative policy freed from considerations of economy alone. It was agreed that specialist committees should not become involved in party political controversy and it was considered that the Select Committee on Nationalised Industries provided an apt parallel to what was intended. The present relationship of ministers to Parliament would not be disturbed: the object of the committee's proposal was "to provide all Members with the means to carry out their responsibilities, rather than elevate any committees of the House to new positions of influence".

The initial government response to the proposal was to reject it as inevitably trenching on policy (in the sense, presumably, of party policy). In a debate in October 1965 the Leader of the House (Herbert Bowden) said that "The real question is whether or not we want to develop a system of specialist committees, not exactly like, but akin to, the American congressional committees and similar committees which exist in certain European countries, or whether we feel that the proper place for policy discussions, as distinct from financial administration, is on the floor of the House. With the best will in the world, I am afraid that ... the necessary detailed examination of government expenditure and administration is bound to give place to policy discussions." But six months later the Prime Minister (Harold Wilson) indicated a marked change of attitude (widely credited to the new Leader of the House, Richard Crossman). He announced that the government was entering into discussions with the opposition "on the suggestion of establishing one or two new parliamentary committees to concern themselves with administration in the sphere of certain departments whose usual operations are not only of national concern but in many cases of intensely human concern" (specific reference was made to the Home Office and the social departments); he undertook that ministers and senior officials would make themselves available to the committees. Subsequently a small number of new select committees were established, some specifically concerned with particular departments (initially, the Ministry of Agriculture and the Department of Education and Science jointly with the Scottish Education Department), and some with a particular subject field (e.g., science and technology, Scottish affairs). Other committees were set up to consider the reports of the Parliamentary Commissioner for Administration (see below, p. 175) and to study the working of the Race Relations Act of 1968.

It is too early to judge the impact of the new committees. The government's intention seems to be that at least the departmentally-oriented committees should each have a limited existence to enable more departments to be covered. One of the reasons is that party managers in the Commons have had difficulty in finding members to man them, and any extension of the system will clearly have profound effects on the nature of the membership of the House, which still permits a high proportion of members to pursue outside careers. But a relatively rapid alternation of departmental committees will make it difficult for members to accumulate that continuous specialised knowledge of the activities of government which for many had seemed the main purpose of the reform. The committees do not seem in practice to have provided any evidence for those who feared that the device would destroy ministerial responsibility or party discipline, although this is no doubt due in part to the fact that the areas of investigation have been much less "sensitive" from a policy point of view than would defence or foreign affairs. The Committee on

Science and Technology first examined the government's nuclear reactor programme before going on to consider defence research establishments, without any immediately perceptible effects on parliamentary debate or government policy formulation or implementation; indeed, when a new government reactor programme was announced several months later it represented a rejection of the committee's main recommendations. The committee examining the Ministry of Agriculture, Fisheries and Food first investigated the possible impact on British agriculture of entry into the European Economic Community. In the course of its deliberations the committee considered that a visit to the Community's headquarters in Brussels would be necessary but it met with considerable resistance from the Foreign Office (anxious about the possible repercussions of such a visit on the government's negotiations for entry then taking place) before it was finally allowed to go. The committee was able to record in its first report, however, that the Ministry of Agriculture itself had been co-operative, if sometimes a little tardy. The report and the evidence published with it (like the report on the nuclear power programme) provided detailed information on a particular aspect of policy which might well not have been made available had the committee not been appointed. This in itself may be thought by proponents of specialist committees to justify the innovation.

Organised Publics

Public accountability has a much wider connotation than the answerability of ministers and government departments to Parliament. Both the formulation and implementation of governmental policy involve extra-parliamentary institutions, groups, and individuals in more direct ways than they do ordinary Members of Parliament who, by the nature of the British political system, are essentially on the periphery of the policy process (specialist committees notwithstanding). What have been variously described as "organised publics", "pressure groups", and "the lobby" here play a vital part since they channel attitudes and expertise in areas in which the government needs to operate. There is a heterogeneous

mass of such groups, all varying in aims, activities and composition, but most classifications recognise a rough distinction
between "promotional" groups (e.g., the R.S.P.C.A., the
Campaign for Nuclear Disarmament, the Howard League
for Penal Reform), which explicitly exist to further a cause
by influencing public authorities either directly or (more
often) through the pressure of public opinion; and "interest"
groups (e.g., the T.U.C. and individual unions, the Con-
federation of British Industry and employers' associations, all
manner of professional associations) whose primary concern is
the interests of their members but which sometimes need to
influence governmental policy in pursuit of those interests.
As a general rule it is the interest groups which exert the
greatest influence, for they often have the resources, the staff,
and the expertise necessary to bring decisive pressure to bear.
And that influence—again because of the nature of the British
political system—is normally most decisive in direct contact
with government departments where policy is implemented
and new policies prepared. Individual M.Ps. can be useful
to the groups, particularly as sponsors of Private Members'
Bills (many of which originate in interest group activity) or
as spokesmen in debates on the various stages of Bills, above
all the detailed committee stage (S. E. Finer has traced the
origin of every significant amendment tabled to the Transport
Bill of 1946–7 to the relevant interest group). If specialist
committees are seen to be influential it may well be that
groups will also try to work through them as American
groups conspicuously do through their congressional counterparts. But for the most part contacts with M.Ps. and generalised
public campaigns are, for the most influential organised publics, supplements to their main points of contact among
ministers and civil servants in the departments.

There is in fact a symbiotic relationship between government departments and many organised groups, for each
needs the co-operation of the other for the fulfilment of their
tasks: the groups need to know about the implementation
and modification of policies which vitally affect them, and
government departments need the expert assistance of the
groups, and the relative ease of consultation with wide

interests which their organisation provides. It is a relationship which, to be effective, calls for discretion and restraint
on both sides. The whole process has given rise to the system
of permanent advisory committees attached to the main
government departments (see above, p. 79), to which interest groups often nominate members and by which they
are, so to speak, institutionalised within the administrative
structure (they are also frequently called on to nominate
members of *ad hoc* commissions and committees of enquiry).
In economic planning, for example, an elaborate consultative system has been created around the National Economic
Development Council set up in 1962. The council itself has
become the main institutional forum for discussions between
the government and leading representatives of industry and
the trade unions, and there is now a whole series of similarly-
constituted economic development committees (or "little
Neddies"), each concerned with one of the major industries.

Organised groups are particularly concerned with the
minutiae of administration, with the details of policy rather
than with general principles, and this requires an intimate,
continuous, and confidential relationship with departments.
Interested groups are consulted before legislation is prepared
and the information they provide is often essential for its
drafting; although the groups cannot be shown the precise
text of the draft legislation before it is laid before Parliament,
they can be made aware of its general intention and, if possible, their assent secured. The officials of the local government associations, for example, see the great majority of
departmental circulars and statutory instruments concerning
local authorities and their work before publication and, even
more important, are consulted about contemplated changes
in government policy, whether to be effected by legislation or
administrative action; the associations are, on the whole,
satisfied that their views are taken into account, while the
departments themselves recognise the value of the advice
they give. Most governmental policies cannot be implemented
without the co-operation of interest groups (e.g., the British
Medical Association and the health service, teachers' associations and the educational system) and in some cases outside

private bodies actually administer legislation as agents of the government (e.g., the Law Society and legal aid, the Royal Society for the Prevention of Accidents and road safety campaigns and training).

The development of close institutional links between organised publics and the administration has not been without its critics. Brian Chapman, among others, has claimed that too often the formulation of governmental policy is seen simply as "finding the least controversial course between the conflicting demands of vociferous private groups". But others see in the fact that groups' interests and demands do conflict (as the interests of the powerful National Farmers' Union, representative of 90 per cent of British farmers, often conflict with those of manufacturing industry) a safeguard against a monopoly of influence for a single group, however powerful. And the reconciliation of conflicting demands which government departments and the government as a whole have continually to undertake in their relations with interest groups may often be the only practicable way in which that rather nebulous entity "the public interest" can be secured. The answer to the excessive influence of particular interests or the under-representation of others is the organisation of more groups, not an interdict on their direct approach to the machinery of government. For it is through them that public opinion can most effectively be brought to bear on the details of the administrative process.

For Further Reading

Arora, R. S., "Parliamentary Scrutiny: The Select Committee Device" in *Public Law* (1967), 30–41.

Beet, E. H., "Parliament and Delegated Legislation 1945–1953" in *Public Administration*, 33 (1955), 325–32.

Butt, Ronald, *The Power of Parliament* (Constable, 1967).

Chapman, Brian, *British Government Observed* (Allen & Unwin, 1963).

Chester, D. N., and Bowring, N., *Questions in Parliament* (Oxford U.P., 1962).

Coombes, David, *The Member of Parliament and the Administration: The Case of the Select Committee on Nationalised Industries* (Allen & Unwin, 1966).

Craig, J. T., "The Working of the Statutory Instruments Act 1946" in *Public Administration*, 39 (1961), 181–92.

Crick, Bernard, *The Reform of Parliament* (Weidenfeld & Nicolson, 2nd edn., 1968).

Parliament and Organised Publics

Eckstein, H., *Pressure Group Politics* (Allen & Unwin, 1960).

Finer, S. E., *Anonymous Empire* (Pall Mall, 2nd edn., 1966).

Finer, S. E., "The Individual Responsibility of Ministers" in *Public Administration*, 34 (1956), 377–96.

Griffith, J. A. G., and Street H., *Principles of Administrative Law* (Pitmans, 4th edn., 1967).

Hansard Society, *Parliamentary Reform* (Cassell, 1968).

Hanson, A. H., and Wiseman, H. V., *Parliament at Work* (Stevens, 1962).

Hanson, A. H., and Wiseman, H. V., "The Use of Committees by the House of Commons" in *Public Law* (1959), 277–92.

Jennings, Sir Ivor, *Parliament* (Cambridge U.P., 2nd edn., 1957).

Johnson, N., *Parliament and Administration: The Estimates Committee 1945–1965* (Allen & Unwin, 1967).

Johnson, N., "Parliamentary Questions and the Conduct of the Administration" in *Public Administration*, 39 (1961), 131–48.

Kersell, J. E., *Parliamentary Supervision of Delegated Legislation* (Stevens, 1960).

Mackenzie, W. J. M., and Grove, J. W., *Central Administration in Britain* (Longmans, 1957). Chapters 20 and 24.

Marshall, G., and Moodie, G. C., *Some Problems of the Constitution* (Hutchinson, 4th edn., 1967).

Morrison of Lambeth, Lord, *Government and Parliament* (Oxford U.P., 3rd edn., 1964).

Normanton, E. L., *The Accountability and Audit of Governments* (Manchester U.P., 1966).

Potter, A. M., *Organised Groups in British National Politics* (Faber, 1961).

Pritchard, E. P., "The Responsibility of the Nationalised Industries to Parliament" in *Parliamentary Affairs*, XVII (1964), 439–49.

Reid, Gordon, *The Politics of Financial Control* (Hutchinson, 1966).

Richardson, J. J., "The making of the Restrictive Trade Practices Act 1956—A case study of the policy process in Britain" in *Parliamentary Affairs*, XX (1967), 350–74.

Ryle, M., "Committees in the House of Commons" in *Political Quarterly* (1965), 295–308.

Select Committee on Agriculture, Session 1966–67: *British Agriculture, Fisheries and Food and the European Economic Community* (H.C. 378 and 338, H.M.S.O., 1967). *Departmental Observations* (Cmnd. 3470, H.M.S.O., 1967).

Select Committee on Procedure, Session 1964–65: *Fourth Report* (H.C. 303, H.M.S.O., 1965).

Select Committee on Science and Technology, Session 1966–67: *United Kingdom Nuclear Reactor Programme* (H.C. 381, H.M.S.O., 1967).

Self, P., and Storing, H., *The State and the Farmer* (Allen & Unwin, 1962).

Stewart, J. D., *British Pressure Groups* (Oxford U.P., 1958).

Walkland, S. A., *The Legislative Process in Great Britain* (Allen & Unwin, 1968).

Walkland, S. A., "'Unusual or Unexpected Use' and the Select Committee on Statutory Instruments" in *Parliamentary Affairs*, XIII (1960), 61–9.

Williams, Roger, "The Select Committee on Science and Technology" in *Public Administration*, 46 (1968), 299–313.

Wiseman, H. V., "Supply and Ways and Means: Procedural Changes in 1966" in *Parliamentary Affairs*, XXI (1968), 10–15.

8. Public Accountability: Judicial Control and Administrative Discretion

It is a truism to say that the British political and administrative system observes no clear separation of powers between legislative, executive, and judicial institutions. That term itself, of course, is open to several interpretations, some linking it with a separation of *personnel* in the governmental system, some with a separation of *control*, and some with a separation of *function*. It is the separation of personnel which is most obvious in the major "separation of powers" constitution, the United States, with President and other members of the executive government *ipso facto* debarred from membership of the legislature or the judiciary. But there is no clear separation of control, nor of function, even formally, since, for example, presidential assent is necessary for congressional legislation, the Senate needs to ratify major presidential appointments and treaties, and the Supreme Court, in its role of constitutional interpreter, plays a major role in both legislation and its implementation (e.g., the Court's influence in the civil rights issue since 1954).

Judicial Control and Administrative Discretion

In Britain, ministers—the political heads of the executive—are members of the legislature (as are the most senior judges, the "law lords" in the House of Lords). But there is some separation of personnel between legislature and executive since civil servants and many other public officials are ineligible for membership of the Commons. The merging of the political leadership of the executive with the legislature makes possible the virtual control of the legislature by the executive; separation of control is seen only—but importantly—in the fact that judges, although appointed by the executive, exercise their functions independently of it. A separation of powers by virtue of function has little practical place in the British system, in common with those of most other modern industrial nations, including the United States. The administration promulgates rules of law in the form of delegated legislation with little or no reference to Parliament, although the authority to do so is usually given by statute; administrative tribunals set up by ministers adjudicate on a wide range of disputed questions, especially those involved in the administration of the social services; courts, by interpreting obscure areas of the law, in effect make law themselves, while some courts make purely administrative decisions (e.g., the granting of licences to publicans). The truth is that power is widely distributed rather than separated and there seems no virtue in attempting to confine functions which are recognisably rule-making, rule-implementation, or rule-adjudication to particular bodies. The doctrine of the separation of powers in a functional sense is so remote from what happens in practice that it may well be "better to disregard it altogether" (Griffith and Street).

Judicial Control

Dicey's classic formulation of the related concept of the Rule of Law also needs revision in the light of the situation which has developed since the first edition of his *Introduction to the Study of the Law of the Constitution* in 1885 and which was well in train (as Dicey himself later recognised) before Dicey's death in 1922. All persons—including officials in the exercise of their duties—are still formally subject to the ordinary law interpreted by the ordinary courts, which give the aggrieved citizen remedies in cases of dispute with the administration. But a whole range of such disputes are in practice decided outside the courts, perhaps by means of an administrative tribunal or after the holding of an inquiry, but often by a minister or official acting in his name without going through any procedure which allows affected individuals a voice. In what ways, then, is it still possible to talk of administration under the law, of judicial control of the administration?

The courts are able to take action on behalf of a plaintiff against an official of the administration if the plaintiff is able to show (1) that the official has failed to carry out a legal obligation or (2) has acted without legal authority, i.e., *ultra vires*. In the first category the doctrine that "the King can do no wrong" was applied formally until 1947, and was deemed to cover ministers and officials acting in their name. The complicated procedure of a "petition of right" had to be gone through to impose liability on the Crown for breaches of contract; in tort (i.e., civil wrongs other than breach of contract) the Crown could not normally be sued at all, but only its servant, appearing as a private person, who had committed the tort (e.g., a post office van driver injuring a pedestrian). The Crown Proceedings Act of 1947, for the most part, assimilated proceedings against the Crown both in tort and contract to the procedure of one citizen against another.

Ultra vires actions are relatively frequent against local authorities and their officials since they are circumscribed by law in a much more obvious way than central government (see Chapter 6). Thus in 1921 Fulham Corporation was prevented from providing a municipal laundry under its statutory power to provide baths and washhouses, and in 1955 Birmingham had to suspend its scheme for allowing free travel for elderly people on the city's transport services until an Act subsequently legitimated travel concession schemes already in being. But they can also be brought against ministers and departments—for example, in cases of delegated legislation (e.g., that brought against a 1954 order by the Home Secretary providing for certain changes in the boundaries of parliamentary constituencies), or against ministerial or departmental decisions (e.g., the delay which the education minister was obliged by the High Court to observe in September 1967 before his amended rules for admission to an Enfield grammar school could come into effect). The judicial remedies available include *injunctions,* to restrain the commission of some specified act, *declarations,* giving a formal statement of a plaintiff's rights, and the prerogative orders of *mandamus* (commanding a public authority to perform one of its public duties), which is one of the legal sanctions which central government can bring to bear on defaulting local authorities, *prohibition* (prohibiting an authority from continuing a process contrary to law), and *certiorari* (an order removing the record of the proceedings of a lower court—which for this purpose includes an administrative tribunal—into the High Court so that the court can do what is right, e.g., quash a decision arrived at in excess of jurisdiction).

The courts make a distinction between purely executive duties conferred on a minister, where the grounds on which he acts are left entirely to his discretion (e.g., the naturalisation of aliens), and those which involve "arbitration" or "having to adjudicate between two or more parties", which must be carried out "judicially", in accordance with "natural justice"; for if a minister is enjoined by statute to act judicially and it can be shown that he has not done so he has thereby acted beyond his statutory powers, i.e., is *ultra vires.* Under both these heads, however, the courts have, in general, shown reluctance to be drawn into pronouncing on the merits of disputes with the administration, especially where matters of policy are involved. In consequence the courts have in general seemed to lean rather more towards the executive than towards the individual plaintiff: either by deciding that certain decisions are entirely discretionary, even when, for example, they are preceded by a public inquiry (as in the Stevenage new town case in 1948), or by interpreting the requirements of natural justice in a sense liberal to the executive (as in the famous case of *Arlidge v. the Local Government Board*, 1914–15, where the House of Lords disclaimed any attempt to prescribe judicial forms for a ministerial arbitration, in this case the consideration of a local authority's compulsory purchase order for some of Arlidge's properties).

Tribunals and Inquiries

It is the growth of the welfare state which has been primarily responsible for the tremendous twentieth century increase in "administrative justice". The administration of social services throws up numerous issues of a "justiciable" character, such as the determination of whether a certain elderly person is entitled to a pension or of what constitutes a fair rent. Where there is a more or less settled body of administrative rules (e.g., pension regulations) the process can most nearly approach that of a court of law, i.e., the application of law to the facts; where it requires the ascertainment of facts in order to lead to a ministerial decision related to administrative policy, the judicial element is obviously much smaller. For the first of these categories the appropriate instrument of decision-making is often an administrative tribunal, appointed by the appropriate minister but in practice having a high degree of independence, since it is working within settled policy; for the second, statutes may prescribe some kind of inquiry as a preliminary to a ministerial decision.

A tribunal has obvious advantages over a court of law for the settlement of disputes arising in the often highly technical implementation of modern social and economic legislation, covering such matters as social security (e.g., national insurance and industrial injuries local tribunals), the health service (e.g., the N.H.S. Tribunal, service committees, medical practices committees), land and property (e.g., local valuation courts, agricultural land tribunals), transport (e.g., licensing authorities for public service vehicles), and taxation (e.g., the general and special commissioners of income tax). Tribunals are, in general, cheap, speedy, expert, and flexible. But since they operate in widely differing fields there has been, at least until recent years, a great variety in their personnel (e.g., as to whether any member had legal qualifications) and procedure. Some did not publish the evidence on which their decision was based, some held hearings in private and did not allow legal representation, and from some there was no appeal to a court of law, even on what was explicitly a matter of law. The holding of statutory inquiries is even further removed from the atmosphere of a traditional court of law. Many are held in connection with the compulsory purchase of land by local planning authorities. The typical procedure is for a ministry inspector to preside over a private local hearing or a public local inquiry, with the acquiring authority and the objectors giving evidence, perhaps represented by counsel; if the inquiry is public, other interested parties may also be heard. The inspector then makes a report to the minister, who has not normally, until recently, made the report available to the parties. The minister, advised by his officials, then makes his decision, which may be based on policy considerations quite removed from the evidence submitted at the inquiry, as in the designation of Stevenage as the first new town under the New Towns Act in 1948.

Despite the repugnance of many common lawyers to this development, most trenchantly expressed by Lord Hewart in 1929 in his *New Despotism*, Britain seemed to be acquiring, haphazardly and *ad hoc*, a complex system of administrative courts reminiscent of French "droit administratif" (which Dicey in the 1880s contrasted unfavourably with the British situation), but one which lacked the central control exercised over the whole French system by the highly competent and authoritative *Conseil d'Etat*. In 1955 a group of Conservative lawyers, in a pamphlet entitled *The Rule of Law*, called for the establishment of a special administrative division of the High Court to supervise the whole field of administrative justice, including minister's discretionary decisions. In the previous year the Crichel Down affair, although quite unrelated to the question of administrative jurisdiction, seemed to confirm many people's fears of the existence of "administrative lawlessness". These two events together prompted the Conservative government to appoint a committee under Sir Oliver (later Lord) Franks to consider and make recommendations on (1) statutory tribunals other than the ordinary courts, constituted by ministers or for the purpose of their functions; and (2) administrative procedures which include the holding of an inquiry or hearing by or for a minister on an appeal or as a result of objections or representations (terms of reference which thus excluded the Crichel Down type of situation where officials were guilty of maladministration but where there was no statutory procedure for holding an inquiry).

The Franks Committee published its report in 1957. The committee believed that both statutory tribunals and administrative procedures involving inquiries should be characterised by "openness, fairness and impartiality"—in other words, the rules of natural justice. But it recognised that these characteristics could not be present in the same way or to the same extent in all the procedures. There is an obvious difference between tribunals and inquiries. Members of a tribunal are neutral and impartial in relation to the policy of the minister, except in so far as that policy is contained in the rules which the tribunal has to apply; tribunals are properly to be regarded, in the committee's view, as "machinery provided by Parliament for adjudication rather than as part of the machinery of administration". But when a minister is deciding cases coming to him after an inquiry he has to apply a departmental policy and in this sense is not, and cannot be, impartial. In general the report concluded that despite the haphazard way tribunals had developed, this method worked reasonably well, but that inquiry procedures needed to be as open as possible just because they end in decisions taken by a minister or departmental official. The committee regarded both procedures as "essential to our society", but it emphasised that in "deciding by whom adjudications involving the administration and the individual citizen should be carried out preference should be given to the ordinary courts of law rather than to a tribunal unless there are demonstrably special reasons which make a tribunal more appropriate, namely the need for cheapness, accessibility, freedom from technicality, expedition and expert knowledge of a particular subject". Similarly, preference should be given to decision-making by a tribunal rather than a minister, and this meant that, wherever possible, policy should be expressed in the form of regulations capable of being administered by an independent tribunal. But where a tribunal was set up or adjudicating functions entrusted to a minister the ultimate control in regard to matters of law should be exercised by the traditional courts: the committee did not believe that the case for a separate administrative court had been made out.

The principal general recommendations of the Franks Committee were, as regards *tribunals:* tribunal chairmen should be appointed by the Lord Chancellor, who would also be responsible for the removal of members; chairmen of tribunals should ordinarily have legal qualifications (while tribunals which hear appeals from other tribunals should always have legally-qualified chairmen); hearings should be in public with legal representation permitted, save in exceptional circumstances; decisions should be fully reasoned; and rights of appeal to the High Court on points of law should be extended. On *statutory inquiries* the committee recommended that the procedure should be altered to give all interested parties adequate prior notice and a fuller indication of the case they had to meet; and inspectors' reports should be published. The committee also recommended that two Councils on Tribunals (one for England and Wales and one for Scotland) should be established to maintain a continuous review of the constitution and working of tribunals (and appoint their members), and to exercise certain advisory functions in relation to statutory inquiries.

The government speedily announced more or less complete acceptance of seventy-one of the ninety-five recommendations in the Franks Report and modified acceptance of others, and proceeded to implement them by legislation (most importantly, the Tribunal and Inquiries Act, 1958) and by administrative action (e.g., the Ministry of Housing and Local Government circular no. 9 of 1958, which essentially implemented the recommendation about the publication of inspectors' reports). The Tribunals and Inquiries Act established, not the two Councils on Tribunals recommended by Franks, but a single council, with a Scottish committee (since many tribunals operated throughout Great Britain), appointed jointly by the Lord Chancellor and the Secretary of State for Scotland.

The Council on Tribunals has fifteen members, all part-time, including one appointed primarily to represent Welsh interests and, since 1967, the Parliamentary Commissioner for Administration *ex officio* (see below, p. 176); its Scottish Committee has eight members, four of them not members of the main Council. The Council's functions are:

(1) to keep under review the constitution and working of specified classes of tribunals (numbering over 2,000 individual tribunals);

(2) to consider and report on matters relating to tribunals referred to it by the Lord Chancellor or Secretary of State;

(3) to make general recommendations to the appropriate minister as to the making of appointments to tribunals or to panels from which tribunal chairmen may be drawn (under the Act the appropriate minister is responsible for appointing both tribunal members and chairmen, but the latter he appoints from panels maintained by the Lord Chancellor, whose consent must be obtained before any tribunal member can be dismissed);

(4) to be consulted before any order is made by the Lord Chancellor or Secretary of State which would create an exception to the general rule that both tribunals and ministers making a decision after a statutory inquiry must give reasons for their decisions;

(5) to be consulted before regulations are made prescribing procedure to be followed by a tribunal or at a statutory inquiry (the inquiry function was given to the Council by the Town and Country Planning Act, 1959);

(6) to consider and report on statutory inquiry procedures referred to it by the Lord Chancellor or Secretary of State "or as the Council may determine to be of special importance" (thus while the Council does not have the general surveillance over inquiries that it exercises over tribunals it can raise matters on its own initiative).

Subsequently, the Tribunals and Inquiries (Miscellaneous

Tribunals) Order, 1965, brought within the Council's general supervision a number of additional tribunals, some of which had been in existence a considerable time, and in the following year the Tribunals and Inquiries Act, 1966, extended the Council's functions relating to inquiries to those inquiries which ministers are not statutorily obliged to hold but which they may hold at their discretion.

The general view is that since it started work in 1958 the Council on Tribunals has "performed actively and efficiently within the limits imposed by the Act" (Griffith and Street). It is a purely advisory body, with general oversight over tribunals and inquiries but without the function of appointing tribunal members; it is not in any sense a court of appeal, still less a *Conseil d'Etat*. Government departments normally consult it when drafting legislation, creating new tribunals, or altering the jurisdiction of existing tribunals, but not when drafting legislation involving public local inquiries; nor is the Council asked whether particular issues are best decided by the ordinary courts, by tribunals, or by inquiries. The Council's annual reports have shown that its main concern on procedural rules for tribunals has been with such matters as legal representation, notification of reasons for decisions, and fair hearings. The Council gains direct knowledge of the working of tribunals by sending its members to attend hearings and has made special investigations of particular types of tribunals (e.g., rent tribunals). It also receives on average about fifty complaints a year from members of the public about the working of tribunals or the conduct of inquiries, and takes them up with the appropriate departments. The majority of complaints deal in fact with inquiries, where the Council's role is more restricted than in the field of tribunals. It was, however, in relation to inquiry procedure that the Council scored perhaps its most notable triumph when, after it had published a special report on the so-called "Chalk Pit case" in 1962, the government revised the rules about reopening an inquiry when a minister has received fresh evidence after the conclusion of an inquiry (the Council was less successful in getting official recognition of the rights of third parties, which were also at issue in this case).

Whatever its usefulness the Council on Tribunals is limited in its operation to one sector only of the enormously wide field over which administrative decision-making impinges on the ordinary citizen. It is concerned with administrative decisions which must be preceded by some more or less public procedure in the form of a tribunal or an inquiry. But many discretionary decisions are taken in the almost inviolable privacy of a government department. And even when there is some form of public inquiry it is often difficult to resist the conclusion that official policy has already been firmly determined in advance and is highly unlikely to be radically revised in the light of anything which may emerge at the inquiry. Many felt this, for example, of the inquiry which preceded the designation of Stevenage as the first new town and of that which in 1967 led the government, against the findings of the inspector holding it, to confirm the decision to develop Stansted as London's third airport (although, in response to public pressure, the government later agreed to hold another and much fuller inquiry). The traditional political restraints of parliamentary question and debate (or even the vigilance of a free press) are too arbitrary in their operation, largely because, as was seen in the previous chapter, information about what decisions may require investigation is lacking. Major policy decisions get the publicity of the ordinary political process: the real problem is presented by the multiplicity of "sub-political" discretionary decisions which, covered by the tradition of ministerial responsibility and Civil Service anonymity, largely elude outside scrutiny.

The Parliamentary Commissioner for Administration (Ombudsman)

It was this latter field which was examined in an authoritative but unofficial report, *The Citizen and the Administration*, published in 1961 on behalf of "Justice", the British section of the International Commission of Jurists (the report is usually known as the "Whyatt Report" after its principal author, Sir John Whyatt). The report pointed out that the terms of reference of the Franks Committee had precluded it from inquiring into that large area of administration in which the acts and decisions of officials acting for ministers are not subject to any independent check other than that which is provided by Parliament. Consequently the committee was unable to give any consideration to the question of whether any discretionary decisions which do not at present come under the tribunal system could be brought within it; nor to the question of acts of maladministration, such as occurred in the Crichel Down case where officials showed bias and unfairness in their dealings with the public. The Whyatt Report itself reached two broad sets of conclusions on these questions:

(1) That there was substantial scope for subjecting a large number of administrative decisions involving discretion (e.g., those recommending the remission of import duties, the allocation of new telephones, the supply of certain medical benefits, the choice of a school) to some kind of appeal if there should be a complaint by an individual affected that a decision was not the right one in the circumstances. This, the report suggested, should come from an extension of the tribunal system under the general surveillance of a more powerful Council on Tribunals.

(2) That new machinery was required to deal with complaints of maladministration, i.e., "complaints that an administrative authority has failed to discharge the duties of its office in accordance with the proper standards of administrative conduct". The report paid tribute to the high standard of administration of government departments and the relative infrequency of major mistakes (a view presumably based on general impressions rather than empirical data). There seemed to be, however, "a continuous flow of relatively minor complaints", not sufficient in themselves to attract public interest but of importance to the individuals concerned, who were often frustrated by the apparent inadequacy of existing means of seeking redress.

The report then examined some of these existing means. In some cases of maladministration judicial remedies were available, but these involved the expense of litigation (for those not qualifying for legal aid) and the litigant was faced with "the limitless resources of the State", prepared, if necessary, to take the case on appeal to the highest court. Parliamentary procedures were not nearly comprehensive nor detailed enough for the task. The *ad hoc* procedure under the Tribunals of Inquiry Act of 1921 is only rarely utilised— seventeen times since the Act was passed—and then only on the initiative of the government of the day, usually in response to political pressure. The chief value of these investigations has been derived not so much from the redress of grievances—the issues are often party political ones—as from the detailed light they sometimes throw on particular administrative processes (e.g., the 1957 Bank Rate "leak" tribunal, the 1963 tribunal on the Vassall spy case).

The remedy the report proposed was the introduction of an official on the lines of the office of *Ombudsman*, or parliamentary commissioner for grievances against the administration, which had been operating successfully in Scandinavian countries and which was being introduced in New Zealand (under the title of *Ombudsman*) at the time the report was published. The British *Ombudsman*, or Parliamentary Commissioner, should enjoy the same status as the Comptroller and Auditor General; he would be answerable only to Parliament and irremovable except at the request of both Houses. He should be given wide powers (subject to ministerial veto) to investigate and report on cases of alleged maladministration by government departments (and later, perhaps, by local authorities), initially at the request of a Member of Parliament, but later members of the public should be able to take their allegations and complaints direct to him. He would have access to the correspondence on departmental files, but not to internal minutes, and his reports would not name individual civil servants.

Despite the obvious attempt in the Whyatt Report to make the *Ombudsman* proposal palatable to those who disliked institutional change, especially when based on a foreign model, the government reply, when it came over a year later, was wholly negative, both as regards the tribunal system and the appointment of a Parliamentary Commissioner. The government considered, the Prime Minister (Harold Macmillan) told the Commons in November 1962, that there were serious objections to both proposals, and it would not be possible to reconcile them to the principle of ministerial responsibility to Parliament. Any substantial extension of the system of reference to tribunals would lead to inflexibility and delay in administration and the appointment of a Parliamentary Commissioner would "seriously interfere with the prompt and efficient dispatch of public business". The government believed that there was already adequate provision for the redress of any genuine complaint of maladministration, in particular by means of the citizen's right of access to M.Ps.

Although thus rejected by the Conservative government the parliamentary commissioner idea was taken up by the Labour Party in opposition and found a place in its 1964 election manifesto. A year after the Labour government came to office a White Paper was issued, and in February 1966 a Bill to establish the office was published. The measure finally became law in March 1967, after a good deal of amendment in the course of the debates, and the Parliamentary Commissioner for Administration (Sir Edmund Compton, a former Comptroller and Auditor General) and his staff officially began work on 1st April, 1967. At the same time a new Commons select committee was established to examine the reports of the Parliamentary Commissioner, on the analogy of the Comptroller and Auditor General and the Public Accounts Committee (on the same analogy the chairman is a member of the opposition).

In some ways the office created by the Parliamentary Commissioner Act of 1967 represents an advance on the carefully-guarded proposals of the Whyatt Report. In his investigations the Commissioner has access to all the departmental files (including internal minutes) and cannot be denied information—as can the courts—by a claim of Crown privilege: but the Commissioner is subject to the Official Secrets Acts and ministers have power to prevent him disclosing information where matters of security arise. The Whyatt Report also recommended that a minister should be able to veto an investigation by the Commissioner but this restriction was not included in the Act. Otherwise there is a close similarity between the Whyatt proposals and the actual powers of the Parliamentary Commissioner. Those powers are limited both in function and in area of operation. Above all, the Commissioner is concerned with only a small part of the whole range of discretionary decisions by departments— those which give rise to complaints of "injustice caused by maladministration" (roughly defined by the Leader of the House during the Commons' debate on the Bill as including "neglect, inattention, delay, incompetence, ineptitude, perversity, turpitude, arbitrariness"). The emphasis is on procedure rather than the decisions themselves. The Whyatt Report had proposed that the question of disputed decisions, as opposed to complaints of maladministration, should be covered by an extended tribunal system supervised by a strengthened Council on Tribunals. No action has been taken on this proposal, and it would seem in any case more appropriate to consider it as an extension of the Parliamentary Commissioner's work than to give it to an entirely separate institution (although the link between the two has been recognised in the appointment of the Parliamentary Commissioner as an *ex officio* member of the Council on Tribunals). This view has been taken by the Select Committee on the Parliamentary Commissioner which, in its second report, published in August 1968, recommended that the Commissioner should, in effect, be concerned with the quality of decisions as well as with the procedures attending them.

The Commissioner is confined to cases involving central government departments, and even here is excluded from such fields as the government's international relations (a restriction which in 1968 was held by the government to cover the investigation of the withdrawal of British passports issued to Rhodesians), crime investigation, State security, legal proceedings, and the prerogative of mercy. He cannot investigate local government (except in cases where a central government department is responsible), the nationalised industries, the hospital service, the police, personnel matters in the Civil Service and the Armed Forces, or cases where there is a remedy in a court or tribunal (unless he is satisfied that it is not reasonable to expect the legal remedy to be used).

The Commissioner may receive complaints only through M.Ps. and must make his report to the M.P. from whom the complaint came. Whereas the Whyatt Report envisaged this continuing for a five-year period, with the possibility thereafter of direct contact between the individual complainant and the Commissioner, the Act is silent on the point. It was thus not only the doctrine of ministerial responsibility (as in the restriction to cases of maladministration), but also the susceptibilities of M.Ps., conscious of their own traditional "ombudsman" function on behalf of their constituents, which served to limit the nature of the Commissioner's role.

From the Parliamentary Commissioner's first report (covering the first six months of operation) and his first annual report it appeared that Sir Edmund Compton interpreted his terms of reference strictly and was not disposed to widen the practical meaning of "maladministration". "My practice so far (his first report recorded) is to regard the area for my investigation to be the administrative processes attendant on the discretionary decision: collection of evidence on which the decision was taken, the presentation to the minister, and so on. If I find that there has been a defect in the processes detrimental to the complainant, then I do inquire into the prospects of a remedy by way of review of the decision. But if I find no such defect, then I do not regard myself as competent to question the quality of the decision." He subsequently announced, however, that, following the Select Committee's recommendation, he would also concern himself with defects in a department's procedure for reviewing its rules or in the grounds given for maintaining them. During the period from 1st April, 1967, to 31st December, 1968, the Commissioner received 2,189 complaints, of which just over half were found to be outside his jurisdiction. Of the 562 cases taken up and on which there had been a report, maladministration was found in only fifty-seven, or 10 per cent (the equivalent percentage since 1962 for the New Zealand *Ombudsman*—who receives complaints direct from the public, not through M.Ps.—has been of the order of 15 per cent).

In all the cases where evidence of maladministration has been found the Commissioner normally found nothing to criticise in the action taken by the departments to remedy any injustice caused by the maladministration. But a significant clash between the Commissioner and a department was disclosed in February 1968. In December 1967 the Commissioner published a strongly adverse report on the way in which officials in the Foreign Office had rejected the claims for compensation under an Anglo-German agreement by survivors of a wartime concentration camp at Sachsenhausen: the original Foreign Office decision, he said, had been based on partial and largely irrelevant information and had been maintained in disregard of additional information and evidence. The Commissioner had suggested that the Foreign Office should, in the light of the maladministration he had found, review the evidence and take a fresh decision and, if appropriate, make a financial award to the claimants. In February the Foreign Secretary (George Brown) announced in the House of Commons that he had decided to award appropriate compensation (totalling £30,000) to the Sachsenhausen claimants but at the same time he rejected the Commissioner's charge of maladministration, claiming that it was purely a matter of judgement, on which there was no reason to believe that the Commissioner's judgement was any better than that of the responsible minister. The Foreign Secretary then raised (in a way reminiscent of the Conservative government's reaction to the Whyatt Report in 1962) the question as to whether the investigations of the Parliamentary Commissioner were compatible with the responsibility of a minister for the actions of his officials: "It is ministers who must be attacked, not officials (the Foreign Secretary said). The office of Parliamentary Commissioner was intended to strengthen our form of democratic government, but if the office . . . were to lead to changing this constitutional position, so that officials got attacked and ministers escaped, I would have thought that the whole practice of ministers being accountable to Parliament would be undermined."

The Sachsenhausen case was the first to be considered by the Select Committee on the Parliamentary Commissioner, and it began its consideration immediately after the Foreign Secretary's announcement (the committee said in its report that it regretted that this had not been delayed until after it had had an opportunity to report). The committee heard evidence from the Parliamentary Commissioner, the permanent head, and the senior legal adviser of the Foreign Office and two M.Ps. who had been pursuing the claimants' case. The Foreign Office witnesses maintained the departmental position that no maladministration had occurred but indicated (as had the Foreign Secretary), without giving any details, that a review of procedures was being undertaken. The committee reported its dissatisfaction with this situation and its intention to call for further evidence from the Foreign Office "to ascertain what remedial measures have in fact been taken as a result of the review, and to test their effectiveness". In his own evidence the Commissioner was careful not to indicate his personal views about the Foreign Office attitude but he did comment on the position of officials who are investigated. The Act empowered him to identify and report maladministration in a department collectively, including the ministerial level. It was also open to him to blame or exonerate a specific individual. Any official blamed had to be given the opportunity to defend himself in private to the Commissioner and must have a copy of the report of the results of the investigation, which would state the grounds on which the Commissioner found the complaint against him justified or otherwise. It was then up to the minister of the department to decide on (1) whether to endorse or disown the action the Commissioner had criticised as maladministration, (2) the remedy to the complainant, and (3) the remedy in the department. The Act was silent on (3), but if the minister disagreed with the Commissioner on (1) and (2) then the Commissioner had power to make a special report, and that was what he had done in the present case.

The confrontation between Commissioner and a major department which the "Sachsenhausen affair" precipitated (added to the Commissioner's willingness to extend his interpretation of his role) has done much to relieve doubts about the potential effectiveness of the new institution. The incident illustrated the major difficulty which has faced newly-established *Ombudsmen* elsewhere, as in Denmark (from 1954) and in New Zealand (from 1962)—the suspicion of the departments liable to investigation. The Danish and New Zealand officials are now firmly established and there seems no reason to doubt that the British Parliamentary Commissioner, with increased responsibilities, will come to be accepted as a permanent and vital element in the control of public administration.

For Further Reading

Allen, Sir C. K., *Administrative Jurisdiction* (Stevens, 1956).

Brown, R. D., *The Battle of Crichel Down* (Lane, 1955).

Chapman, Brian, *British Government Observed* (Allen & Unwin, 1963).

Chester, D. N., "The Crichel Down Case" in *Public Administration*, 32 (1954), 389–401.

Council on Tribunals, *Annual Reports* (H.M.S.O., from 1960).

de Smith, S. A., *Judicial Review of Administrative Action* (Stevens, 1959).

"Donoughmore-Scott Report"—*Report of the Committee on Ministers' Powers* (Cmnd. 4060, H.M.S.O., 1932).

Elcock, H. J., *Administrative Justice* (Longmans, 1969).

Foulkes, David, *Introduction to Administrative Law* (Butterworth, 2nd edn., 1968).

"Franks Report"—*Report of the Committee on Administrative Tribunals and Enquiries* (Cmnd. 218, H.M.S.O., 1957).

Friedmann, Karl A., "Commons, Complaints and the Ombudsman" in *Parliamentary Affairs*, XXI (1968), 38–47.

Garner, J. F., *Administrative Law* (Butterworth, 2nd edn., 1967).

Garner, J. F., "The Council on Tribunals" in *Public Law* (1965), 321–47.

Gellhorn, W., *Ombudsmen and Others* (Oxford U.P., 1966).

Griffith, J. A. G., "The Council and the Chalk Pit" in *Public Administration*, 39 (1961), 369–74.

Griffith, J. A. G., "The Crichel Down Affair" in *Modern Law Review*, 18 (1955), 557–70.

Griffith, J. A. G., and Street, H., *Principles of Administrative Law* (Pitman, 4th edn., 1967).

Justice, *The Citizen and the Administration* (The "Whyatt Report") (Stevens, 1961).

Marshall, G., and Moodie, G. C., *Some Problems of the Constitution* (Hutchinson, 4th edn., 1967).

Mitchell, J. D. B., "Administrative Law and Parliamentary Control" in *Political Quarterly* (1967), 360–74.

The Parliamentary Commissioner for Administration (Cmnd. 2767, H.M.S.O., 1965).

Parliamentary Commissioner for Administration, *Annual Reports* (H.M.S.O., from 1968).

Judicial Control and Administrative Discretion

Parliamentary Commissioner for Administration, Session 1967–68: *First Report* (H.M.S.O., 1967); *Third Report* (on Sachsenhausen case) (H.M.S.O., 1967); Session 1968–69: *First Report* (H.M.S.O., 1968).

Robson, William A., *Politics at Home and Abroad* (Allen & Unwin, 1967). Chapter 7.

Rowat, D. C. (ed.), *The Ombudsman* (Allen & Unwin, 2nd edn. 1967).

Select Committee on the Parliamentary Commissioner for Administration, Session 1967–8: First Report, *Sachsenhausen* (H.C. 258, H.M.S.O., 1968); Second Report (H.C. 350, H.M.S.O., 1968).

Stacey, Frank, "The Machinery for Complaints in the National Health Service" in *Public Administration*, 43 (1965), 59–70.

Wade, H. W. R., *Administrative Law* (Oxford U.P., 2nd edn., 1967).

Wraith, Ronald E., "The Public Inquiry into Stansted Airport" in *Political Quarterly*, 37 (1966), 265–80.

Yardley, D. C. M., "Rent Tribunals and Rent Assessment Committees" in *Public Law* (1968), 135–53.

Appendix:
Government Changes,
October 1969

Under government changes announced on 5th October, 1969, the Department of Economic Affairs and the Ministry of Power have been abolished. All the functions of the Ministry of Power and some of those of the D.E.A., together with the Board of Trade's responsibility for distribution of industry, have been transferred to the Ministry of Technology which has thus become, in effect, a Ministry of Industry. The title of Minister of Power (to whom statutory duties are entrusted) continues to be held for the time being by the Minister of Technology.

The D.E.A.'s regional economic planning functions, including supervision of the planning councils and boards (see pp. 94-6), have passed to a new minister, the Secretary of State for Local Government and Regional Planning, who also co-ordinates the work of the Ministry of Housing and Local Government and the Ministry of Transport which, for the time being at least, remain separate departments. The full ministerial appointment of a Minister of Planning and Land (see p. 13) within the Ministry of Housing and Local Government has lapsed.

Government liaison with the National Economic Development Council, of which the Prime Minister is chairman, and the National Economic Development Office has now passed from the former D.E.A. to the Cabinet Office, which thus somewhat increases its economic advisory role (see p. 36).

Appendix: Government Changes, October 1969

The changes illustrate several of the themes discussed in the text. The Cabinet has been reduced in size (from 23 to 21), but only by excluding two more departmental heads, the Minister of Housing and Local Government and the Minister of Transport (see p. 13), although their co-ordinating minister (the Secretary of State for Local Government and Regional Planning) will speak for them, as the Minister of Defence did for the Service Ministers from 1946 to 1964 (see p. 27). The greatly expanded Ministry of Technology provides a further example of another device for effecting co-ordination, that of the merged ministry (as with the Ministry of Defence from 1964 and the Foreign and Commonwealth Office and Department of Health and Social Security from 1968).

The changes illustrate also, of course, the problem of distribution of departmental functions discussed in Chapter 3. In particular the disappearance of the D.E.A. marks the end of an attempt to isolate in a special department a function of co-ordinating economic policy distinct from its actual execution (see pp. 45-6). Much of the general economic co-ordinating responsibility of the D.E.A. has now returned, in form as well as in practice, to the Treasury.

Another governmental change preceded the announcement of 5th October, 1969, by a few days. As from 1st October, 1969, with the coming into being of the Post Office Corporation, the historic title of Postmaster General has given way to that of Minister of Posts and Telecommunications. The new minister exercises, in respect of the Post Office Corporation, powers similar to those of other ministers supervising public corporations.

Index

Index

Civil Service, 2-3, 4, 65-86, 93-4, 98-9, 102, 163, 176
— — Administrators and specialists in, 76-8, 80-1, 81-3
— — Anonymity of, 75-6, 85, 145, 172
— — Centre for Administrative Studies, 75
— — Classes, 67-8, 72-3, 80, 81-2
— — College, 83, 86
— — Commission, 47, 66, 85-6
— — Department, 11, 47-8, 62, 85
— — Fulton Committee on, 4, 47-8, 66-7, 69, 74, 75, 76, 77, 78, 79-86, 142, 149, 150
— — Head of the Home, 43, 65, 66, 85, 124, 150
— — Managerial role of, 74-5, 81
— — and Ministers, 7, 68, 69-72, 76-7, 85, 103, 145
— — — organised publics, 79, 158
— — Recruitment, 72-4
— — Training, 75, 83
Clow Differential, 105
Coal Board, National (see National Coal Board)
Colonial Office, 32, 39, 40, 57, 59, 69
Commons, House of (see Parliament)
Commonwealth affairs, departmental organisation for, 32, 57-9
— Development Corporation, 98
— Office, 32, 39, 57, 58, 59
— Relations Office, 32
— Secretary, 23, 55
Comprehensive education, 130-1
Compton, Sir Edmund, 175, 177
Comptroller and Auditor General, 148, 150, 152, 174, 175
Conseil d'Etat, 167, 171
Constitution, Royal Commission on the, 4, 97
Consumer Council, 3
— Councils (in nationalised industries), 112
Coombes, David, 152
Council for Industrial Design, 98
County Councils Association, 137
Courts of Law, 7, 10, 116, 163-6, 167, 168, 169, 171, 176
Crichel Down, 145, 146, 167, 168, 173
Crick, Bernard, 145, 146, 154
Cripps, Sir Stafford, 26, 43
Crookshank, Lord, 14
Crossman, Richard, 156
Crown Proceedings Act, 164
Curzon, Lord, 15
Customs and Excise, Board of, 38

DALTON, Lord, 7, 144
Decentralisation (see Departments, Government, regional organisation of)
Declarations, 165
Defence, Minister for the Co-ordination of, 27, 29
— — of, 23, 27, 28
— Ministry of, 27, 32, 39
— and Oversea Policy Committee, 22, 23, 24
— Secretary of State for, 13, 24, 28, 56
Delegated legislation (see also Statutory Instruments), 163, 164-5
Denning, Lord, 104
Departmentalisation, principles of, 2, 40-2, 88, 122
Departments, Government, 38-86, 98, 101, 102, 113, 116, 119, 124, 137-9, 152, 153, 158-9, 173, 174, 176
— — Internal organisation of, 67-86
— — Regional organisation of, 88-97, 116, 117
Dicey, A. V., 163, 167
Diplomatic Service, H.M., 58, 65, 74
District Audit, 119-20, 128, 138
Dominions Office, 39, 57
Douglas-Home, Sir Alec (formerly Lord Home), 12, 28
Duchy of Lancaster, Chancellor of the, 11, 13, 30
Dugdale, Sir Thomas (Lord Crathorne), 145

ECONOMIC Affairs, Department of (D.E.A.), 5, 10, 11, 32, 36, 45-6, 48, 62, 71, 95, 96, 110, Appendix
— — Secretary of State for, 13
— Planning machinery, 94-7
— Policy, co-ordination of, 42-6
Education Act of 1944, 118, 130
— Committees, Association of, 79
— Ministry of, 48, 50, 51, 52, 77, 93, 130
— and Science, Department of, 32, 39, 40, 42, 52, 53, 77, 78-9, 138, 156
— — — Select Committee on, 156
— — — Secretary of State for, 11, 22-3, 56, 129, 130
Elections, General, 144
Electricity industry, nationalised, 101, 111

186

Index

Index

PRINTED IN GREAT BRITAIN BY UNIVERSITY TUTORIAL PRESS LTD
FOXTON, NEAR CAMBRIDGE